SELF HELP
GUIDE TO LIVING

by Scott Williams

7 Layers of Dirt
Publishing

Published by:

7 Layers of Dirt Publishing
Denver, Colorado 80260

Manufactured in the United States of America

Copyright © 2019 by Scott Williams

All rights reserved. No part of this book may be reproduced in any form, or by any electronic, mechanical, or other means, without permission in writing from the publisher.

Edited by Heidi Haas
Cover and book design by Scott Williams & Heidi Haas
Layout by Heidi Haas

First edition, 2019

Library of Congress Control Number: 2019906962

ISBN 978-1-7335368-0-6 (soft cover)
ISBN 978-1-7335368-1-3 (hard cover)
ISBN 978-1-7335368-3-7 (ebook)
ISBN 978-1-7335368-2-0 (audio book)

Acknowledgments

This book would not have been possible without immense support (and even badgering) from friends and family. It's been a labor of love over many years, and I'd like to take a moment to acknowledge those that helped make this book a reality.

Thank you, first and foremost, to my wife Heidi for all her technical expertise, her support, her willingness to let me write about her, and basically her patience as I pour time and energy into this silly fantastic hobby.

Thank you to Chris Godskesen for all his help with the audiobook. Without him, it'd be a choppy mess of static and background noise.

I'd like to give a shout out to those that were around years ago when this project started, many of whom are probably shocked that I ever finished it. These include climbers from our old Chicagoland stomping grounds and former co-workers – specifically Ian Blakesely for always checking in on the progress and Danielle Nelson for introducing me to NaNoWriMo – where I really got a chunk of the book going.

I'd like to also acknowledge my parents, sister and my Aunt Corky – a woman whose support is truly saintly.

Finally, to my co-working family here in Colorado, my friends, fellow climbers, therapist peers, and everyone who has supported this project, THANK YOU from the depths of my heart. I appreciate all the love.

Acknowledgments iii

Introduction vi

Part One - Knowing yourself 1
   1   Understanding the mind and body 2
   2   Why did I open the fridge? 6
   3   What am I writing about? 12

Part Two - Stress 17
   4   Get a hold of yourself already 18
   5   Meditation and other stress relievers 28
   6   Sh!t Hits the Fan 33
   7   Dat Scwewy Wabbit 39
   8   Counting to Ten 44

Part Three - Finding the Humor in Life 45
   9   Humor in Strange Places 46
  10   I Cannot Believe I Laughed at That 52
  11   Thank You, Drive Through 56
  12   Bring on Bizarre Thoughts 60

Part Four - Love and Relationships 66
  13   1-800-Dial-a-friend 67
  14   I'd Like to Take You Home Tonight 70
  15   Love is a Sledgehammer 74
  16   Now That You're Stuck with Me 82
  17   OK, You're Really Stuck with Me 83

Part Five - Family 87

18 How Am I Not Adopted? 88
19 My dad can beat up your step-dad. 90
20 My father hates poetry 93
21 Why doesn't Nana just die already? 102

Part Six - Fear and Insecurity 104

22 Nobody Really Likes Spiders. 105
23 Ever hugged a wolverine? 110
24 Dracula Has Fear of Commitment 114
25 I hate changing in the locker room 120

Part Seven - Death 125

26 Never saw it coming 126
27 Who knew there were so many choices for urns?. . 130
28 Eulogy open mic night 133
29 I'm dead, and that's the way I planned it 137
30 The afterlife is a rave, so bring your glowsticks . . 141

Part Eight - Religion 144

31 God is hanging out in Cleveland 145
32 Jesus needs a cape 150
33 I have a fork, just need an outlet 153
34 I walk the path, but I think I stepped in something . . 158

Part Nine - Bringing Closure 162

35 Gimme some tongs, I'm making a life salad. 163
36 Bubble wrap this fragile lesson 167

Introduction

The key element in any guide to living, any self-help book, any diet plan or spiritual path, or even competitive game of Uno involves commitment. Without buy-in from you, the plan put forth may as well be written in Sanskrit. However, if you read Sanskrit, that's pretty cool. Enjoy that brainpower and go do some Sudoku. You probably don't need to read any further. Seriously, put the book down and just run around bragging about your IQ, you ass. Let me lay down a couple basic principles to give you a tease on what you can expect over the following chapters. This book does not contain journal space at the end. You will not be hiring a life coach as a result. You may not find your inner you or become one with your good Chi.

I simply wish to pass along my advice to leading a healthy, and so far, happy life to all who wish to share my experiences and observations. I have a degree in absolutely nothing, lead a normal existence, and aside from being able throw a nice curveball, cure myself from hiccups in a few seconds, and do simple math in my head, I have no outstanding talents. What I do have is an upbeat take on life. I don't do "half glass full" kind of thinking, but rather, "fill the glass up and take a drink, refill, repeat" kind of living. I take tremendous pride in the work I do and still believe I am just slightly better than above despite my attempts to strive for improvement. I do a better job each day of minimizing stress. Let me rephrase that. I make the attempt each day, but it doesn't always work. For example - I try to do a better job minimizing the road rage that builds from within when I'm creeping five miles per hour under the speed limit in single lane construction behind a maroon 1998 Oldsmolbuick being wobbly steered by a 4 foot tall grandmother that I simply have to assume is behind the wheel because I honestly cannot see eyes as high as the dashboard. So yeah, I try. I laugh as often as I can (even when I shouldn't). And, above all, I have great friends and a loving family. My life is excellent. Yours should be as well.

In case you haven't read a fortune cookie lately, let me clue you in to life's basic truths. Pretty people get all the breaks.

Paying taxes sucks. And, everyone dies in the end. Is this any reason to throw yourself off a bridge? Perhaps, but not just yet. Should anger and resentment build in you until you up and go postal on your co-workers? No, definitely not. In fact, your daily challenges are the fuel to improve your existence. Getting through a tough day at the office knowing that the weekend brings a reprieve from the grind keeps some of us from taking the swan dive on to the ten o'clock news. And we all share in these same struggles. Even the Pope has basic stresses. That's why he uses H&R Block for his taxes. No kidding. He loses sleep over the whole thing – I swear to…..

The point is that each of us has the opportunity to dive into our own thoughts with a newfound clarity. We have the capacity to see that which makes us happy, mad, jealous, frustrated, elated, or just plain confused. Ever heard the phrase, "Two goats can fill a mountain, but a true man can break walls?" No. Of course not. It's a stupid phrase that make as much sense as half of the self-help crap you could find on the shelves of any bookstore. "Teacher teacher," you ask? "Will this book be better? Will this book push past the cliché, the mindless generic pizzle that holds the same amount of truth as a two-bit fortune teller?" Indisputably yes. Absolutely. Well, no, actually not. But I'll be making fun of it. Oh, and call me professor, not teacher. It sounds cooler. Thanks. If you need more than satire with a moderately profound nugget of truth occasionally mixed in, go find yourself some Oprah time. I only suggest that you finish this book first, because you've already paid for it. And nobody likes a quitter.

How our mind processes information is a complete mystery to me. It baffles me to ponder why we are attracted to different colors, sounds, smells. I'll use the basic concept of clothing to illustrate the point. For virtually every single piece of clothing that has ever been produced, there is a human that has said to themselves, "Yeah. I'll take that look." Don't even begin to tell me you haven't been at the airport watching someone, wondering to yourself how on earth that person chose to consciously pick out THAT as their outfit? But rest assured, somebody is probably asking the same question about you. That isn't any reason to be paranoid. They don't know any better. I think your shirt matches your pants.

Why are some of us linear thinkers and others abstract? I look at body piercings and tattoos thinking "cool," while others think "ouch." It takes more to set some people off and less to calm others down. These personality differences make us the most fascinating creatures around and to a great degree, I'm glad we don't understand how it all works. I'm ever thankful that reactions, preferences, and behaviors are not easy predictable. It makes life interesting to see what makes each of us tick.

Case in point: Some nights when I've had a long day or my wife seems stressed, we practice "happy feet" before going to bed. Let me explain how it works. Start by tightening up your toes, curling them just up to the point of cramping (don't let it go that far or happy feet will surely not be the result). Then relax and wiggle the toes all around while swirling your ankles in a not-too-rhythmic pattern. Then, relax. Let all the stress filter up through the toes, past the ankles, up the leg, and so on through the body. Moments later, I'm able to drift into a state of relaxation and fall asleep for the night. It's simple meditation, but it makes me smile to have happy feet. The way I figure it, if you can't have happy feet, you can't have happy body. I'm not sure when I first started practicing this. And I know it's not ground breaking. But, what I do know is that I sleep better when I do it. My wife gets a laugh at it, and that's always a stress reliever for her, and I function better for believing in a bit of nonsensical behavior. You should too.

And with that, let us begin.

Part One

Knowing yourself

• 1 •

Understanding the mind and body

Your body is made up of 6,812 bones. Technically speaking, these bones are made of really hard stuff and link together with tendons, pulleys, and ligaments that allow us to dance, run, skip, and even do the Hokey Pokey. Alas, our primary focus will be on the wonderful machine that commands these skeletal pieces – the brain.

The complexities of the brain are more difficult to understand than Ozzy Osbourne reading Shakespeare to the remedial English kids. To follow how our brain works, let's break it down into simple sections that we all can appreciate.

1. The Cerebrum – This section of the brain controls memory and emotions. This area of the brain also gets us in the most trouble. 4 out of 5 doctors in a recent poll not actually taken refer to this area of the brain as the "Kenny Loggins – Danger Zone." Or you can look at it this way: Cypress Hill was actually "Insane in the Cerebrum," but nobody really cares.

2. The Cerebellum – Controls body/limb movement and positioning. If you are looking to juggle, it helps to have the Cerebellum working properly. Many a white man has blamed his poor dancing skills on the pesky Cerebellum, but it is not the fault of the brain. Instead, it is fault of Barry Manilow. Don't ask why. We haven't the time for that now. Keep reading.

3. The Medulla and the Midbrain – These wonderful parts help control breathing, blood pressure, eye movements, reflexes and a bunch of other things you really cannot control yourself. As it pertains to your everyday life,

there isn't much you can do except enjoy the fact that this part of the brain exists and move along – all the while breathing…..aaahhhh isn't it nice that it's automatic.

4. The Hypothalamus – Here is what's left: I'm hungry. I'm thirsty. I'm horny. Thank you Hypothalamus.

Please feel free to refer back to the brain's description any time you're wondering which part is malfunctioning again. Most of this information is correct to the best of my knowledge. Of course, there are other aspects of this book I may simply be pulling out of my…..back pocket.

Now that you are brain experts, what can we do with this knowledge? Color, of course. Remember to stay inside the lines.

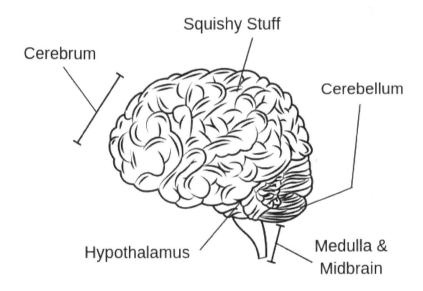

When finished, make a color copy of your brain and mail it to a complete stranger with a note that says:

> "I have lost my mind. Have you seen it? I will pay a large reward if it is found undamaged and uncorrupted. 500 pesos to the first one who returns it.
>
> Brain thief – give it back! I hate you. Just kidding, but seriously, I hate you.
>
> Please write back."

Include a self-addressed stamped envelope and wait to see if someone is courageous enough to reply. If so, you have a new best friend. Or maybe a stalker. You also have to pay the 500 pesos. At the time this was written, 500 pesos was equal to about 240 Egyptian pounds.

Knowing the basics to the brain probably will not have any impact in your daily decisions. People who talk about exercising the brain certainly shouldn't have you piling weights on your head counting off reps. Three more…..two more….one more…. press it out. I haven't heard a single person say to me, "Hey, I was working out my Midbrain the other day. You should see how huge my reflexes are getting." Yet, each day we should exercise the brain. Each part of the brain can be improved and to do so, it needs to be challenged. I'm not saying you should stop reading this and go do a crossword puzzle, but it wouldn't hurt. Just about every activity aside from plopping yourself in front of reality TV helps the brain. Sports not only work the body but can work the mind as well. Remember, your muscles don't move on their own. You can't hold that yoga position without some brain power. Reading a book, solving puzzles, or even video games can help keep the brain stay active and healthy. Here's a sample list of activities from which you can choose to challenge your brain.

Warm-up

1. Simon Sez (the original big electronic circle version)
2. Memorize every line to your favorite movie
3. Badminton (reflex training)

Deep thinking

1. Read (and understand) anything written by Chaucer
2. Put together a piece of furniture from IKEA without instructions
3. Do long division in your head – 389,127 divided by 243

Freaking Mensa level thoughts

1. Ponder how Flavor Flav ever got his own shows
2. Ask yourself, "What would I do without thumbs"
3. Justify the money you spent on this book to a friend

Pacing is everything. Don't overwork your mind or you'll end up with a brain cramp. A charlie horse upside the head isn't good for anyone, so take it slow and work your way up. Don't try to understand why women always have to go to the bathroom in groups, or how men can sit through an entire conversation without hearing anything. These are topics for greater minds and will only cause headaches that fester right behind your left eye for hours. Leave them be.

As the brain goes, so goes the body. The body is fueled by the food you eat, the beverages you drink, etc. How you treat your body has a dramatic impact on the mind, which has an impact on the body, which affects the mind and thus the body? – a perpetual cycle that affects our decision making, our outlook and perspective on everyday occurrences and routines. I know that you certainly understand this, but like many things we claim to know, it's often taken for granted. I certainly do not want to preach about what foods to eat or activities to stay away from. Everyone that has means (and that's everyone reading this book) should eat healthy, find a lifestyle that fits your needs, and treat your body well. Stop juggling knives. It's a stupid hobby that impresses no one. Binge drinking should be done between the ages of 18-20 only. Once it's legal, it's no fun. And if you're between 18-20 and you are going to binge at a frat party, get yourself a morally righteous friend who frowns on that sort of thing who will begrudgingly take your sloppy ass home at the end of the night instead of leaving you on somebody's front lawn. That's about all the advice I have regarding what goes into your system.

• 2 •

Why did I open the fridge?

Ever step into the kitchen, open up the fridge, stare for a minute at the jar of dill pickles with only one left floating there all lonely and such.......then wonder, why did I open the fridge? I'll tell you why. You were looking for the scissors in the left side top drawer that your wife sent you for a couple minutes earlier. This is a condition known as Short-Term Mental Impressionitis. The brain is sensitive to short term memories. As sensory preceptors input data to the brain, its mapped systems filter these images (impressions) to the appropriate channels. However, under stress, swelling appears in the brain cutting the path of the preceptors and rerouting the stimuli to other areas including past memory channels. Based on the strength of the memory, the likelihood that the stimuli are routed toward that memory increases. This condition is much more common in men as we are simple creatures that filter stress more directly to the brain. We don't know any better and therefore are powerless to prevent it. What I'm saying is that it is not our fault. Sorry anyway.

In this next section, we will discuss a related, yet distinctively different type of condition. Actually, I will discuss it, and you will just read. This book is not interactive, nor is there an on-line chat hosted by me in which we share our opinions regarding segments of the book. Do you think I have that kind of time or money? Why did you even bother bringing it up? Seriously.

Of course, I'm talking about ADD (Attention Deficit Disorder). It affects 9 out of every 10 people worldwide, I think. Maybe it's less, but I really don't know. Along with ADD, we have related conditions of ADHD, PCP, and MTV – all of which are serious conditions with equally intense acronyms. How exactly this condition affects us is unknown as not a single scientific study has ever been fully completed. Many get started, but for some reason, scientists veer off in another direction before we figure it out. Oh well. I'll detail a few scenarios and show you ways to combat this affliction. First thing to do is focus your attention and turn the page.

Hey! Turn the page.

FOCUS!!!!

Remember what we're still talking about? Hell, do you remember what book you're reading? Good. That's a step in the right direction.

ADD effects people in exactly the same manner as the common cold apart from a runny nose, potential sore throat, cough, and loss of appetite. Otherwise, it's the same. Not really, but sort of. Many of us wonder if we have ADD. Fortunately, there is a test available to help diagnose the condition. You will need the blue crayon that you used to color in the brain earlier.

ADD Self Diagnosis Test

Please select the appropriate answer to each question.

1. When watching television:
    a. I forget what I'm watching during commercials
    b. I cannot remember what channel I was on if I've flipped too many times
    c. I watch reality TV
    d. I curse that fact that I have a dish and not digital cable

2. When picking out clothes to wear for the day:
    a. I pick from the pile laying on the floor
    b. I coordinate my outfit to match my socks
    c. My spouse/significant other tells me what to wear
    d. Sometimes I forget to put on pants

3. I can concentrate without fail for:
    a. 5 seconds at a time
    b. 5 minutes at a time
    c. 1 hour at a time
    d. There was this one time when I went of a field trip to New York and I met this homeless guy who was asking me for a dollar, and I was like, "Dude. I'll totally give you a buck." Hey that guy looked just like my Uncle Frank. He was always hammered at holiday dinners.

4. My resting heart rate is between:
    a. 50-60 bpm
    b. 60-70 bpm
    c. 70-80 bpm
    d. Orange

5. (Please take two minutes to close your eyes and envision all the different types of birds you can think of. List them off in your brain, but do not write anything down)

How many birds did you can up with?
    a. Bird bird bird. Bird is the word
    b. Birds of a feather flock together
    c. A bird in the hand in worth two in the bush
    d. More than 5

6. I can remember my mother's birthdate.
    a. True
    b. False
    c. Maybe
    d. None of the above

7. When picking out something to read, I am most likely to choose:
    a. War and Peace
    b. USA Today
    c. People Magazine
    d. Screw that - I'm watching Law and Order reruns

8. My hobbies include:
    a. Chess
    b. Sudoku
    c. Counting ceiling tiles
    d. Premeditated acts of questionable morality

9. Some people have called me:

a. Absent minded
   b. Space cadet
   c. Lackadaisical
   d. Jim

10. I have the patience to:
    a. Sit through John Tesh's greatest hits album
    b. Thread a needle blindfolded
    c. Ponder why we no longer have tails
    d. Get through this damn quiz

Great Job! Let's take a couple minutes to grade this quiz. Please give yourself 1 point for every question you answered A. Give two points for each question answered B. Take off 3 points for each question answered C. Give four points for each question answered D. In addition, take off 1 point for each question you answered within 5 minutes of reading it. You should be rewarded for your focus and attention. Tally all of this up and check your score.

Below 10 Points – Unlikely you have ADD. A score this low usually represents several answers of C, which means not only did you take the quiz, tally your score with additions and subtractions, but also that you had the attention to continue to figure it all out. Be thankful this affliction has not found you.

11-20 Points – Very likely you have ADD. The down side is that you probably haven't even read the book this far let alone remember that you had to tally up a score.

21-40 Points – You certainly have ADD. The fact that you know your score falls in this range simply tells me that someone had to help you stay on task. There is no way that you managed to finish the quiz without aid and motivation. Hire this person, and give them permission to slap you back to attention when necessary.

Above 40 Points – Actually impossible. Not a chance you have ADD. Faker! I'll bet you just want the attention and sympathy. How dare you! I'll bet you're the type of person that preys on the weak and afflicted. Nobody likes you, face it.

• 3 •

What am I writing about?

Total concentration is an interesting concept. On occasion, I can engross myself in daily tasks without giving in to temptation of idle conversation, internet surfing, or simple diversions that prevent me from accomplishing tasks at hand. The problem is the ineffectiveness of the in-between. Even now in the course of writing this sentence, I find myself distracted by my wife watching television, my cat hanging out on the couch just behind my head, and the fact that I forgot to brush my teeth this morning. Actually, I didn't really forget. It was a day off from work, and it feels good sometimes to rebel against conformity and social acceptance that says I need to brush my teeth every day.

I guess what I'm saying is that I know me. I understand that this process will be slow. I accept that I will be derailed from time to time. That doesn't mean I like the fact that I struggle with attention issues. I also have moments that I can process information so quickly that I think the world is moving slowly around me. It's those days where I lay my head down on the pillow with a smile to all that was accomplished during the day. How does all this help you? Good question.

Perhaps we need to focus on how well YOU operate. How well does your brain stay on the tracks? It's not a question of ADD, ADHD, or any other diagnosis. You most certainly do not need a doctor to figure this out. I'm just guessing here, but I'd bet that many of us feel like we aren't as productive as we should be. Maybe it's a lack of motivation at work, poor sleep, bad relationships, or too much medication. I blame it on clowns. They're creepy and nobody likes them much. What's your scapegoat?

You need to understand how you process info. Do you

have to write everything down because there isn't a chance of remembering otherwise? Do you use some type of technology or just rely on others to clue you in to the fact that it's your mother's birthday tomorrow? Organization in the brain is quite simple to understand and much more difficult to execute. If you cannot remember phone numbers, birthdates, events, you need to have an outlet to help store the data. Use a smart phone, life coach, day planner, and stick to it. The brain knows where to turn to find the data assuming the data will be there. The problems occur if that info isn't recorded somewhere. And post-it notes don't count.

It's difficult to stay organized in the mind. Think back to the brain diagram. Do you remember which part of the brain controls memory? Of course not. That was like at least 6 pages ago. No need to feel ashamed. I don't know either, and I wrote this damn thing. Keep your focus on the fact that we all need some assistance logging all the details in this information driven world of today. And if you think things are getting simpler, you'll quickly be in for a rude awakening. I read in the National Enquirer – now hear me out on this before you pass judgment- I read that by the year 2020, hard drives will be installed into our brains to help us store all the data to which we are exposed each day. And little USB hubs will be hard wired behind our ears to make our memories and thoughts transferable from person to person. Or, as some believe, it's a ploy by Apple to upload music straight to your brain. Call it iHead. Seriously, this is where we are headed. The good news is that you'll be ready.

Have you noticed all the drug commercials on TV these days? Everyone, it seems, is suffering from ailments we used to classify as people's characteristics. Apparently, there are no more pissy people in the world. Now, they suffer from clinical depression. Well, yah! They are pissy. Ever know somebody that was all fidgety? Nope. That person probably suffers from "restless leg syndrome." And to use the word "suffering" when you have dry eyes is a bit of an exaggeration. If these commercials are true, we either cannot "get it up", are depressed (probably cuz we can't get it up), have anxiety issues, or suffer from gas, problems peeing too much, high blood pressure, degenerative bone structure, advanced aging, acne, halitosis, or some other horrid condition which is only curable with medication that has more severe side effects than the original condition. Did you know there is sleep medication advertised with the side effect of insomnia!? Who the hell is buying this crap? I know marketing is slick, but come on. That's like buying a plunger that's prone to clog your toilet up if used. Sorry for the potty humor.

While we're talking commercials, if you listen carefully, you'll hear a list of symptoms to prove that you need said medication being advertised. Here's a typical scene from any drug commercial:

Cue dramatic music

Announcer: Do you sometimes feel tired? Do you ever have trouble sleeping? Have you ever had a headache or sore feet? Do you ever forget things? If you answered yes to any of these questions or even if you didn't, Zapcroft is for you.

Now before you can ponder the complex stupidity of the question, the commercial continues with a testimonial.

Paid actor posing as not a paid actor: I used to get the occasional headache, but then I heard about Zapcroft once a day pills. Now I don't have to worry about feeling anything. I'm numb for 24 hours at a time with Zapcroft.

It's at this point in the commercial where you first contemplate stabbing the person nearest you in frustration. But the commercial continues before you can release your violent impulses.

Announcer: Ask your doctor if Zapcroft is right for you.

Sorry, I need to interject just for a second. Just what doctor would prescribe this torture on anyone? This is why I go to the doctor as little as possible, and when I must go, I choose the emergency room. That way I am guaranteed to be waiting for at least 6 hours before being treated. This gives me ample time to decide whether immediate medical care and treatment are necessary. And while I'm waxing on about doctors, I don't visit medical establishments to tell THEM what to prescribe. I prefer to leave decisions of that sort to the professionals. Let's continue. After all, Zapcroft still has the rights to the next minute of air time.

Announcer: Side effects may include cramps, chest pain, ocular bleeding, hives, bumps, mumps, chills, heebie jeebies, creeps, creeks, shingles, bowel instability, or death.

> *Author's note: While I was in the process of editing the book after finishing the first draft, I thought the above sentence read "bowel insanity," not "instability." I thought that was even funnier. I thought about switching it, but then you'd never understand what can be found, even in your own thoughts.*

This is the world we live in. And did you notice that at no point is it stated just what Zapcroft can rid you of? Save your money. Save your body. There certainly are some of us that actually need medication. Your doctor, with whom you should take the time to build a relationship, can help you if necessary. But for most of us, it's just life. Deal with it. As a buddy of mine often jokingly said, "I'm a schizophrenic, and so am I." So are you, so are we, and so it shall be.

You're not perfect. To be brutally honest, you're not even close. Me neither, who knew? I can live with that assessment of myself. I still want to drop some weight, and if I find the motivation, it'll happen. I've accepted that I have a gap between my two front teeth. It's not David Letterman big, but it's there and maybe there was a time where I was self-conscious of it. I wanted to get it fixed somehow because I wanted to look better, fit in, and not hear wind whistle through that gap every time I said the word "scissors." That was then. I rarely worry about the little things now. And not worrying about the little things is a big thing.

There's a difference between accepting traits, habits, or characteristics of one's self and simply giving up on the hope of change. If you are cranky and mean seemingly all of the time, that's largely your problem. There are likely people dealing with far worse that are doing far better. Maybe they are simpletons. Maybe ignorance is bliss. If that's true, perhaps you should be simple, be ignorant. You can order up a self-lobotomizing kit from Amazon and get to it. Here's the link: www.amazon.com/labotomy=done=easy=3s5t2%&ilis*#11681681321@55135.

You need to change your focus. Is it as easy as that? YES! It's as easy as that. Keeping the focus is the difficult part. Knowing that you're a crab-ass should be quite obvious. Similarly, if you don't like your appearance, do something about it. Find the will power, put on running shoes and repeat after Forrest, "I just felt like run-in." But be realistic. It's dangerous to push past the point of self-improvement and into compulsion. Some characteristics can be altered, but if you go all-in on the plastic surgery or bake tanning, there comes a line you cannot uncross.

Part Two

Stress

• 4 •

Get a hold of yourself already

Each day brings with it pressures and expectations. Stress can be a real killer if you let it. Part two of this book focuses on the impacts of stress in our lives. I'll outline ways to help process stresses, control and minimize them, and turn them into positive conditioners. Dealing with stress is an everyday occurrence. There isn't an end goal where the stress disappears, but rather an ongoing battle to keep focus and perspective along the way. Sounds stressful, eh?

Let us now examine what causes stress. What exactly is stress for that matter? I'm sure that many of you have heard that there is good stress and bad stress. This is true, or at least you can make it so. Stress is caused by just about anything that doesn't come effortlessly to us. Stress comes from outside circumstances thrust upon us and from the circumstances we bring upon ourselves. How you ever taken a stress test? It's typically a series of questions regarding events that cause stress in everyday life. You rack up points for having characteristics defined by the test to be stress indicators. Your cumulative score is measured in a generalized, judgmental way that says you are basically a ticking time-bomb heart attack candidate if your score is above "X." It should be obvious to you without having to tally up the score whether you suffer from a substantial amount of stress. And regardless of the results, there is often little advice for how to lower the level. If you lose loved ones or your job, if you aren't healthy or you were just attacked by a shark, your stress test score will be off the charts. If you have a happy family, good life, and just had an all-day spa treatment, you still have stress. Certainly, it's easier to manage daily stress when the circumstances are generally positive. This is why I have taken 14 minutes to develop a new scientific stress test that can accurately pinpoint your stress level. After that, we'll filter through ways to deal with our stress.

Stress Test

Directions: Please mentally answer each question, and then read through the discussion section. Pause between questions to reflect on what nerf is made of.

1. Do you have children?

Discussion: If you answered yes, your stress level is already higher than those without. Regardless of their age, you live with the subconscious need to worry about their safety and well-being. This is okay, but you need to realize how little say you have in the matter. The electrical outlet is begging little Johnny to bring over a fork and test it out, and you can't watch him 24/7. Do your best to minimize the damage, kiss them on the forehead and hope for the best. However, if your kids are little brats or have made you broke with a second mortgage to pay for a college education they will throw away by majoring in philosophy, cut ties immediately! Sell them on the black market while they're young and still have value or move away with no forwarding address the minute they're dropped off at the dorm. You cannot afford this level of stress. For goodness sake, this is only question 1. If you answered no, well wooptie freakin doo for you. Aren't you special?

2. Are you in danger of losing your job each day?

Discussion: If so, you are probably a screw-up. You know this, so it shouldn't stress you out much. For reasons unknown to anybody, you'll have no trouble finding other work so you can repeat the process and thus cause stress to future employers that will no doubt question their screening processes once they're terminated your employment. The only other rational explanation to answer yes is that you work in the tech field. In that case, you're screwed. Sorry.

3. Do you have serious medical issues?

Discussion: If not, do your best to keep it that way. Many so-called "doctors" say that exercise is a good stress reliever. If this is true, then you have no good excuse not to stay fit. Eating healthy is another big step. Start balancing out that diet of yours. For example, after eating White Castle, don't go out for ice cream. That's just irresponsible. On the other hand, if you are taking medication for a serious issue, keep on keeping on. That's a huge stress not only for you, but for those who care about you. Seriously, no joke there. I may be going to hell already, but I don't need to catch the express train. On to question 4.

4. Have you ever lost a family member in a blimp accident?

Discussion: I'm just damn curious. If so, email me at self.help.living@gmail.com and tell me all about it.

Have you figured out what nerf is made of yet? What if we started making everyday items from nerf? Like shoes for instance...........WAIT. This just in. What are Crocks made of? Nerf perhaps? I smell conspiracy.

5. How much do money/income/bills stress you out?
    a. Every waking moment.
    b. Every so often when my checking balance is low.
    c. Only when I look at how long it'll take to pay back my student loans.
    d. My wife/husband handles the bills. If the credit card works, I'm okay.

Discussion: This is simple.

Answering A is not as bad as you'd think. You may need to sell yourself on the corner from time to time, but you might actually like that. Remember to get the money up front and it's hard out there for a pimp. Otherwise, put in an application for a night server at Denny's and kiss sleeping goodbye. The other option is to put yourself on a budget, understand that you probably own way too much crap anyway. Stop spending money to look like you have money you do not and get out of debt. It'll take years, but you probably got years to give. Quit stressing over it.

Answering B means you've developed the nice habit of spending just enough to not realize where it went other than the fact that the amount you just put in your gas tank matches to the penny the amount left in your account. Interesting coincidence, I think not. It isn't until you get an alert on your phone reminding you that your math skills don't account for services charges on your CHASE Freedom account. And though you have overdraft protection, it isn't applicable to monthly service charges and now you owe an extra $20 that you really don't have. You could alleviate this problem by making coffee at home each morning and saving the $4.44 spent on a Starbucks venti Café Mocha.

Author's note: I'm on my second Starbucks drink sitting here right now. No bull. Hypocrite, I know.

Author's follow up note: The first author's note was while I was writing the book. Fast forward a couple years and I am now enjoying a cookie something something frappuccino. Still a hypocrite.

Answering C most likely means you've been practicing solid money management skills. I'll bet that you've already been through answers A and B at some point and have learned from your mistakes. Good for you. I'm sure it's a bit less stressful. I bet you even have a fluffy pillow and sleep well at night. No need to flaunt it. You still have student loans and no rich family member to bail you out. If somebody was going to pay your way through college, they would've stepped up by this point.

I know there isn't a single person reading this book who answered D to this question. This type of person should be slapped. "My SUV that I didn't pay for doesn't fit in the parking spaces…wah wah wah blah blah blah." In fact, it stresses out everyone else to know you exist. Damn. I need another Mocha!

6. Choose the answer that best describes you. I sleep:
    a. only a few hours at night though I may lie there for upwards of 8 hours.
    b. better with a body pillow or somebody to snuggle with.
    c. pretty well unless I'm stressing out over an issue.
    d. therefore I am.

Discussion: Most of us will answer A, B, or C. If we allow stress to interfere with our sleep habits, it'll carry over into the next day and the day after in a cycle. You need to find a way to make sleep a valuable tool to energy renewal and preparation for the upcoming day. This section of the book will delve deeper into this topic. If you answered D, you are one cool cat. You don't stress the mess. And, as *the hipsters say, "That's quite a bag of bread." Dig it.*

7. I relieve stress by:
    a. Smoking
    b. Eating
    c. Watching TV
    d. Playing video games

Discussion: On the surface, these may not seem like the textbook "good" answers. I'm sure you were ready for me to throw in reading, meditation, yoga, etc. The truth is that I don't think there are too many bad answers to stress relievers – everything in moderation, though. I think chain smoking your way through the daily grind will not help you for very long. Eating yourself huge will not go unnoticed. But, if you cannot bring yourself to silent chant or downward dog, fine. I'm not saying you should go that route. But you do need to find a way to decompress when life throws stress at you. I purposely left drinking out of the mix the first time I went through this question. Then I decided that it needed my attention. Is drinking a good way to relieve stress? Sure. Who the hell am I to tell you differently? Would I recommend it? Nope, probably not. I stick with the thought of things in moderation. If you down a couple beers and unwind, okay. If you down a couple beers five nights a week, harbor resentment toward your children that you take out on your spouse…..well, you got issues.

8. Are you happy with your life?

Discussion: Wow. This is a loaded question that could drag out for chapters or even whole books. As it pertains to managing daily stress, I offer this simple suggestion. Find the aspects of your life to which you can answer the question with a yes, hold on to them, and try to adjust more areas to the yes column. But one at a time. Trying to look at everything at once is often the source of the stress in the first place. You may need to shake some things up to get there, which causes uncertainty, fear, anxiety, and more stress. Keep your focus on long term, and you should be better off.

9. What color would you associate with stress?

Discussion: I know you chose red. Okay, you're a rebel and you chose black. Don't try and tell me you chose any other color. Here's what I want you do. Mentally associate stress with mauve, pink, or beige.

Not as stressful anymore, is it? That's the power of the brain. Close your eyes, take two long deep breaths. Decompress for a moment. I don't care what's going on right now. Do it. If you don't feel better, do it again. I swear this works. Ten bucks says your shoulders and neck feel a bit better. (If I'm wrong, I'm not paying up. Hope that doesn't stress you out.)

10. Last question of the stress test. Are you going to continue your life without adjusting to improve its quality?

Discussion: If you dare answer yes to this, come by my house. I will be happy to slap you. Otherwise, you're already moving in the right direction.

Stress tests help point out what we already know. Life is tough, and though we have control over many aspects, we don't have the ability to magically set ourselves up in a fairy tale scenario. The economy sucks from time to time, and we may find ourselves out of work with high gas prices or lose a loved one when we weren't expecting it. We can't just make lots of money with a snap of our fingers or always be in a healthy relationship. Heck, sometimes our pets don't even like us. It's these moments where I fall back to the best quote that has ever stuck in my brain. Its author is unknown making it even cooler to me. I think it would great if it turned out to be some part time fortune cookie factory worker with a fresh outlook. Anyway, here it is:

"Peace is not the absence of conflict, but the ability to cope with it."

I've never heard it put better. Playing baseball in high school, many of us wrote sayings inside our ball caps; motivational little sayings like 'pride' or 'courage' or 'discipline.' I wrote this little mantra across the bill of my cap. Now I wasn't the most popular ball player, writing Zen-like motivational quotes instead of monosyllabic etchings like 'kill,' but it was clear to me even as a teenager that this quote was as well written a statement as I was bound to come across for a while. As an English major, I spent much time reading. For every great piece of literature I read, I scanned my eyes across a few musings that would be better served wiping my butt. That's a bit harsh, I know. But the reality is that there is certainly plenty of published word floating around that proves only that the printing press was a cool invention.

Is this book any different? I submit that it is – should you want it to be. I believe that managing stress starts and ends with your perspective. If you stress over the little things, how can you hope to deal with the real stresses? Allow me to give you an example. You're at a restaurant for lunch. The waitress saunters over to take your drink order and you ask for a Coke. She apologizes and tells you they have Pepsi products. What is your reaction? Based on my personal observations, you will most likely lose your F***ing mind! Holy crap the world is ending because they don't have Coke. This is what I talk about when it comes to perspective. The poor waitress is standing there taking abuse from you because it's somehow her fault that your jacked-up taste buds prefer one chemically charged caramelized beverage over another. It's in this moment that you become the soft drink connoisseur snob that is so offended that the thought of partaking in a Pepsi product to be the equivalent of having someone take a dump in your mouth. Think I'm exaggerating? Ask around. I know people that will LEAVE the establishment to get the preferred product elsewhere rather than "subject" themselves to what they consider such a hideous alternative. If this situation ruins your day, you have to get a grip. And stop looking around right now as if it might not be you. I know this bugs too many people. You're guilty. Accept it, and adjust your attitude. If you wonder why you're having a heart attack at 55 years old, this is why. If you are shaking your head saying to yourself, "I usually just have water," good for you. Shut the hell up. I'm just proving a point.

Need another example? Okay. Let's talk about road rage. Oh, look at you turn red with guilt. Is there anything more stressful than bumper to bumper traffic? For those that have a work commute over 30 minutes, you know all too well what emotions come out of us during heavy traffic. I know many of you spew venom directed at other drivers that would make a potty-mouthed sailor blush. As I sit here in peaceful bliss, I am almost ashamed at the words I've strung together to describe my frustration in traffic. And why do we let this become overwhelmingly stressful? It's not as if we didn't expect it. Ever get stuck in traffic or road construction and wonder why everyone's moving slowly? Nope. We know exactly what a "road construction ahead" sign means to us. Even now as you read this, your stress level just went up half a click thinking about it. Now imagine this. In the middle of gridlock, you look over to the car merging in next to you and you see a person completely oblivious to the situation. They look as happy as a clam as they jam out to a song on the radio. You roll your window down in disbelief to hear that they are singing Purple Rain at the top of their lungs horribly out of key, but with a fervor that rivals Prince live in concert. They turn to you as if you're the audience of this solo concert, rip their rear-view mirror right off, use it as a microphone and keep belting out the song as they merge just in front of you. Your reaction might be to think they're out of their mind. I'll bet it stresses you out a bit more and maybe pisses you off a bit that they don't seem affected by the traffic. It almost angers you more that they don't share if your traffic misery. Damn them. That should be you! Practice by taking the first opportunity you have to find your guilty pleasure song and sing the crap out of it out regardless of who's around – unless you like country music. If so, keep it to yourself. Nobody wants to hear that shit.

Finding perspective allows us to categorize stresses as we encounter them. Think of it this way. We'll classify stresses into three levels.

Level one stresses are everyday inconveniences that will find resolution within moments or certainly by the end of the day. These are minor disagreements, small distractions, and mild irritants. Examples such as mildly upset clients or customers, misplacing keys for a few minutes, or a small stain on your shirt come to mind. If you cannot let this little stuff go almost instantly, you've got to seriously work on perspective. I'll hazard a bet that also says that if you struggle with this, you have a temper and a reputation for losing your cool. Don't be an a-hole. Adjust your perspective. It'll blow people's minds.

Level two is the stress that you should notice. The more you can throw into level one, the better. But not everything can, or for that matter, should be dismissed. Level two contains more long-term stresses that are often related to life planning and direction. These can include moving toward career goals and relationship goals. This probably includes personal appearance and self-image stresses as well. Most of us want to look good and be successful. I personally want to be wealthy. Being rich sounds nice, but I don't stress over it. I've carved out another path for myself that likely won't intersect with monetary prosperity. That's cool. I dig my life. You should too. Keep these stresses in check by doing what you can with what resources you have. If you cannot afford or justify a health club membership and personal trainer, don't sweat it (hah. It was when editing that I noticed how punny that was). Don't mutter to yourself about what great shape you'd be in like the celebrities that can afford it. Instead, put your efforts into carving out a couple feet of carpet space in your living room and get going with those sit ups and pushups. Let's take it a step further. If you work two jobs scraping out a living, and you come home a few nights a week too exhausted to get in a workout and you need to toss on reality TV for a half hour to let your brain relax, okay. Don't stress over the fact that you aren't working out. But if that half hour turns into 2 hours of Survivor and reruns of House and you eat fast food for lunch and dinner, then you have bigger problems to deal with. And no doubt that stress is eating away at you. Fix it, and fix it fast. Tomorrow can be a better day.

Level three contains the only stresses that really slow you down. We're talking death, sickness, or long-term care of family and friends. We're talking career lay-offs and serious illness. We're talking fire or hurricane sweeping away your home. These stresses cannot be pushed nonchalantly aside, nor should you try to do so. Deal with these stresses using all the help you can get. This is exactly the time to pull out favors from friends, lean on family, take help and handouts. Go through all the emotional processes so you don't allow these stresses to linger and bring in other problems. Stresses of this magnitude can be the cause for relationship break-ups, drug dependency, long lasting depression and other unnecessary complications. My lovely wife read this paragraph and suggested I get witty and write some clever closing to finish the section on a happier note. She mentioned that the book can be serious without being a downer. I agree with the notion but lack the creativity to always carry out the execution. The reality is that stress is truly difficult and sometimes the truth cannot be disguised with humor. Maybe this chapter needs to end on a down note. Maybe it's better that I don't always throw a smart-ass comment to defuse the message.

This may be over simplifying stress, but as I see it, perspective lies with perception.

• 5 •

Meditation and other stress relievers

Let's chat a bit more about stress reduction. As I write sections of this book, I'm using my friends as guinea pigs. Many of them get a kick out of reading pages hot off the presses, feeding my ego, and thus the book motors on. A few of them stopped after reading the original outline to ask if I'm going to discuss meditation as an aid to stress relief. The answer is yes, but probably not in the fashion that first comes to mind. I'll define meditation as any mental process that serves to bring perspective and peace to the body and mind, reducing stress and anxiety. I like that definition and since it's my book, that's the definition we're sticking with.

Our minds and our personalities have built-in safeguards than are difficult to penetrate. I believe that most of us are raised to be skeptical to anything that puts us in a vulnerable position. We fear looking silly, getting publicly embarrassed, or opening up to unconventional exercises. Me too. I have less inhibition than some, but I am secretly envious of those that are willing to jump at the chance to experience just about anything. Here's a great example. I don't get on the dance floor at weddings without a couple drinks in me. Even then, it's rare that I will wander past the outer perimeter. It stresses me that I may show the world my inability to keep anything resembling rhythm. I have friends on the other hand, that probably dance worse than me that stumble out center stage to showcase their epileptic dance moves to all. The point is that they embrace their inner goofball. They are enjoying life for what it is, and I'm stressing out at a table drinking red wine. Sounds backwards, doesn't it?

Let's use that as a transition into stress reduction. If you can become that person on the dance floor, you'll be open to the following suggestions.

Suggestion #1:

When you feel stress building up, you need to head it off as early as possible. You can focus on simple breathing exercises as these might be the easiest quick fix to simple stress. The key as I see it is to release while exhaling. I know that sounds redundant, but when I say release, I mean expel not only the breath in your lungs but the feelings and stress that are bugging you. Everything should wash away if only momentarily. There isn't a single better way to momentarily find balance in one's self than to take a deep breath or two and release it all. You'll notice that I didn't use the deadly "R" reword. I said release, not relax. Nobody likes to be told to relax. For whatever reason, it implies that you're a lunatic who could be set off at any moment. So just to be clear, I told you to release, okay? Damn, would you just relax? ♩ Close your eyes, hum, and take a moment for yourself. If anyone asks what you are doing, let them know that you are clinging to the bit of sanity that remains before the voices in your head take over.

Suggestion #2:

Lose yourself in music. I personally like thrash metal as much as anything. I discovered in college that played at ear bleeding levels, I could use metal music to either hype me up or to help me take a much-needed nap. The louder it got, the more it drowned out the world and I found peace. I admit the rest of the dorm floor did not share in my taste. Oh well. I apologize to those that had to deal with my roommates' wonderfully loud stereo. I hope they found peace somewhere else. Currently, I am listening to music from LesMes. It all depends on the mood. Music is a powerful force that can invoke emotion, so use it to your advantage. Please avoid listening to music that will reinforce your stress. If you have a "wallow in self-pity" playlist chocked full of sappy ballads, you get 15 minutes max on that playlist. No more than that. Got it? Good. And while we are at it, no Lou Bega music. Seriously, no.

Suggestion #3:

If you feel that work is just a daily grind, then suggestion 3 might help. Even if you enjoy your job/career, you wouldn't say no to improvement. Assuming you work a typical 8-10 hour shift, you need your breaks to be breaks. There isn't anything wrong with being productive during a lunch break, but I believe that if you spend your lunch break racing around to take care of chores only to jump straight back to work without some sort of decompression for you, it adds to the stress level. I don't think you need a half hour of yoga mat meditation or a mid-day nap, but you need some time. It may be ten minutes in the backroom reading people magazine or just an extended bathroom break. Either way, find a few minutes of undistracted "you" time. Remember to breath. Be conscious of it for a moment before you head back to the grind.

Suggestion #4:

Get a hobby. Take up skeet shooting. I don't care. You'll find meditative qualities spending time with a hobby that brings you joy. Hobbies allow us an escape and it's not solely measured in the time with which we participate in the activity. Just having a time slotted to get away from the grind allows us to maintain a positive attitude in anticipation of our upcoming hobby. Knowing you get to go bowling on Wednesday, catch a movie on Friday, or see a friend for dinner later this week can change our entire perspective on the days preceding. Without this, our daily routine seems quite pointless.

Suggestion #5:

Embrace daydreaming. Children are blessed with the ability to explore a limitless imagination. As we grow older, we come up with excuses and rationalizations for why we cannot continue this behavior. You need to get it back. If you can unleash the mind, you'll find a world of exciting thought that does not revolve around daily responsibilities and worries. Find a friend and pose nonsense questions to one another and then answer them seriously. Example question: If I had to pick one animal to take into combat against a gang of surly monkeys that threatened to take over New York by shooting coffee beans from their belly buttons, what animal would I take? Answer: Giraffeapotomus, of course. With their long necks and tank-like bodies coupled with the love of coffee beans, we would soon make friends with the monkeys and instead work together to build an urban playground with a coffee bean landing surface that kids could enjoy, and parents could get fresh ground coffee. It's what's known as a "win-win".

If that's too silly for you, well, exactly. That's what I'm talking about. We drag the daily stresses around with us each day. It's important that you take the time to shed them before attempting to rest for the next day. I believe that if we all practice similar rituals just before bed, we would wake happier and healthier. Just think, it could be a kind of club with simple rules that we all belong to at night. We could call it "Night Club." And the first rule of Night Club is that we never talk about .... wait, never mind.

All Chuck Palahniuk jokes aside, we certainly will be better off as a collective whole if everyone had the chance to start the day off truly refreshed. If you're interested in meditation and mind cleansing, you can experiment with different types of relaxation techniques. Some people listen to the sounds of water or whales or babbling brooks or babbling whales or trees crying or some crap like that. I like the traditional approach of working the stress out from toes on up or head on down. I'm sure most everyone has tried this at one time or another. Feel the stress leave your feet as they grow heavier and heavier. Feel the stress leave your legs and your knees. Feel the stress leave your thighs as you sink into peace, etc, etc – all the way up to your head. And then you drift off to a peaceful slumber. Sometimes it's easier if someone is talking you through it. It certainly helps if they have a soft soothing voice. I believe it would just be simpler to record James Earl Jones talking you into a trance. James, if you're reading this, think about it! There's some huge money to be made there. We could call it "James Earl Jones sings a lullaby".

For many people, deciding to relax just isn't that simple. Ever been lying in bed at night trying to get to sleep when you realize your partner is still wound up from the day's events? For those that haven't experienced this, it means that as long as your partner is restlessly stirring, you aren't likely to get much sleep. In fact, you quite quickly become an active participant in the process. I know some of you are shaking your head no, no, no. I will go to sleep when I want. Let me enlighten you. If you don't want to be spending the next couple nights on the couch getting that sleep, you best wake back up and learn to be a good listener.

And if she is particularly on edge (yes, I said she), please refrain from telling her to calm down or using the "R" word. Do you remember what this word is? I referenced it just a couple pages back. If you cannot remember what it was, find a female and ask – very, very nicely.

In other words, not many of us cannot just turn off stress at the end of the day. We come home after a long day to more of life's other stresses – kids, bills, relationships, responsibilities, and it seems as if there isn't any break. At the end of the day, sometimes dropping from exhaustion is the easiest solution. Personally, I would suggest avoiding sleeping pills, alcohol, and other drugs. Not only are they bad for you, addictive, blah blah blah, but they're expensive. Seriously, with the cost of gas these days, who can afford good drugs?

On occasion, we need that a bit of meditation during the day or during a particularly stressful moment. Each of us needs what crazy people refer to as your "happy place." Once again, it can be as simple as a taking a deep breath or for some, it's a noon nap. Just make sure you have your woobie.

Sh!t Hits the Fan

What are we to do when shit hits the fan? Remember when you were younger and everything was a life and death situation? Envision a 2 year-old, trying to wrap their head around the fact that the parent is not buying them a toy from the store. My my how a child can throw a blood curdling scream-fest of a tantrum because to them, not having that toy is everything in which their world revolves. From an adult's view, we have perspective. And, we kind of want to slap the kid. It's fair to admit. You're not gonna do it, but you want to. Don't say you didn't think it. As we grow older, these problems are replaced with the newer causes of stress such as social acceptance and appearance. The first time we have a crush on someone and we realize it isn't going to work out, our lives are over. The drama unfolds, and it is years later that we come to understand that perhaps getting so worked up over a crush was a little unnecessary. Besides, it probably wouldn't have worked out between you and your fifth-grade science teacher. I'm just guessing.

So naturally we need to learn from these moments and foster a better perspective. Our emotions do a marvelous job of clouding our objective judgment, but they are not without value. Without them, apathy would take hold and we wouldn't care about what was happening to us. Heck, if apathy set in now, I wouldn't even bother to finish this sentence, or even take the time to……………..whatever.

I had one of those "sh!t-fan" moments recently at work. I first tried to make sure I didn't freak out or get too emotional. As the day dragged on, I was able to gain perspective and my stress level decreased a bit. I still wanted a stiff drink after work, but I instead called those close to me to see how they were doing. As it turns out, my problems were not only much like theirs, but in many ways, no big deal upon comparison. Nothing makes you feel more like an a-hole than when you're complaining to someone with real problems. "Yah it sucks that your mom is really sick in the hospital, but can you believe that we're like two people short in our marketing department?" Like I said, makes you feel like a punk, doesn't it?

Make no mistake, I am writing this book for me as much as you. I still stress about work situations, but for the most part, I'm not taking it home any more than necessary. I found perspective quickly in that last situation, and that is something that would have been more difficult in the past. I use my friends and family as support just as you do. I still vent to my wife as she does to me each evening. We try to always pick out the positive points of our day, but some days can be tough. Everyone needs the chance to bitch a little bit, though I think people like to complain far too much. I bet if you think quickly, you can come up with more than a couple people you know that thrive on negativity. These are the same people that love to add to a negative conversation. We need to start a reality competition. We'll get two people together and watch them one-up each other's negative comments. It's like the bitchy version of watching two guys compare childhood war wounds. "Oh yeah, well I fell off my bike when I was eleven, and I got fourteen stitches across my forehead. The scar's pretty much faded." "Oh yeah, when I was seven, I wrecked on the jungle gym and my head popped off. Swear to god. My parents had to have it sewn back on, but I still played outside that afternoon." That's pretty much how it goes. I'm not exaggerating as much as you might think.

I hope you enjoyed that little tangent. I'm not sure what I'm trying to say except that when times get rough, we have to understand that in most cases, practically all cases, life has a way of working itself out if you can find the focus and perspective to not make the situations worse. Focus on the areas with which you can have an impact. Don't let yourself carry excessive worry about the areas that you cannot really control. Here are a couple great examples in today's economy.

Situation #1:

Gas prices keep rising. I'm sure many of you cannot affect the gas prices directly by yourself. Focus on what you can affect. Buying a fuel-efficient car makes sense. Carpooling makes sense. Driving a bit less makes sense. These are areas you directly control. So rather than stress over the price, do what you can to take some control over the situation. That is of unless you live 50 miles from you job in the far suburbs in a new housing development in a house way too big for what you needed but it sounded great because the price was cheap and so you bought an SUV because it was trendy and you need a vehicle that could double as a monster truck for a family of only four but now you realize you can't sell your home because the housing market is shot and your company is tossing rumors of layoffs at you because you work in the tech field and the job market is shrinking in a post dot-com boom society. If that's you, I'm sorry. Go ahead and stress out. You're kinda screwed for a while.

Situation #2:

You don't have a job, or you know soon you might be out of work. You need to start thinking about the next job. The word career means less and less these days. Company loyalty means even less. A job is a job is a job. There are places that are hiring. I swear it. Hell, I'm hiring at my job right now. It's a question of pride much of the time. This is especially true of those who have more training and schooling. I don't take too many hard stances on subjects, but this is one I feel clear about. If you don't have work, you can find it somewhere. First swallow the pride, realize that it is just a job, and then focus on finding something else that might be more suited to your abilities. My parents worked their butts off with multiple jobs before I was born and though my childhood years to pay for continued education, a good Christmas for my sister and I, and simply so they could make ends meet. I'll be flipping burgers tomorrow if I need to do it. Walmart greeter? Hell yeah. Bring it on if it'll pay the bills. We are not defined by the work we do unless we want to be. And if that is the case, I think you're missing out in life. That's just my opinion. And I'm right about it.

Life is going to bring times that leave many of us wondering how the hell am I going to get through this? How am I going to pay for this, do that, find time to get this done, etc.? Somehow, it usually gets done. Otherwise you'd see people spontaneously combusting on the sidewalk. Sometimes people almost romanticize about the hopelessness of their situation simply because it's clear that the way out of the pickle is through self-sacrifice and hard work. We all want the quick fix. That's why you see so many "bankruptcy made easy" commercials at night.

Not that you know it, but this book is in a state of constant revision until I finally just break down and wrap it up with a pretty ribbon. I keep coming back to previous chapters to add little sections. Here's a perfect example. I fly for business every few months. On the way to Memphis from Chicago, I had the privilege of flying in the exit row. Bonus for me, more leg room. For those that haven't flown in this row, you have the responsibility of assisting in the case of an emergency landing. You are also required to give a verbal confirmation that you can assist in these responsibilities should the situation occur. On the way back from Memphis just two days later, I again was seated in the exit row. Could fortune smile upon me twice? I submit that it can. This time I was asked, and I'm paraphrasing, if I could assist in ripping off the 45lb emergency door and chucking it out the side while escorting flaming victims to safety, I gave a resounding, "Hell yeah" to the flight attendant. She was less than amused, but I thought it was funny, so whatever. I was seated alone on my side of the row, working on my computer when in the middle of the flight, we suddenly experienced what I thought was turbulence. My computer shot across the tray table hitting the side wall and it felt like we were hanging a hard left at 500 miles per hour. Then plane dropped, my stomach rose, and suddenly everyone was at attention. Within a couple minutes, we got the good news.

"Attention everyone. This is your captain. We crapped the muggle haven kop a top, blen hookd the blevle rumaton."

I couldn't make out a damn thing he was saying, and by the confused look of the other passengers, I wasn't the only one. He then continued.

"Blah diggity then blum. Something something rebbish gum tucknugget. *We've lost auto-pilot.* Simplu fleg ham doppitlund."

Whoa. Back that shit up a bit. We've lost auto-pilot!? What does that even mean? So we're all a bit shook up by this point. The plane is now silent. When the captain returns to the PA system, we're all at attention and we can hear him a bit better. He explained that there was a malfunction and the extent of the complication is unknown, but in layman's terms, we had no power steering. If you've ever driven a car without that, you know it's a bitch. If you have to land a plane without it, well, damn.

So he asks if anyone aboard is a firefighter, police officer, etc, and before I know it, they've escorted a gentleman to join me in the exit row seat. I asked him if he was a firefighter or something and he replied, "I'm the guy they call in these situations." I was thinking, *Awesome, he's either MacGuyver or they got an Air Marshall on board.* Secretly, I was hoping for MacGuyver. Either way, I felt better. The captain told us we'd make it to O'Hare, but we'd be making an emergency landing – hopefully on the runway. He had everyone follow through the entire emergency landing procedure card, and believe me when I say that everyone was reading along like perfect pupils in school. He continued with the cheery news that it was very likely that upon landing (at least he didn't say crashing), we'd likely be making multiple impacts. Depending on how well this ordeal was going, he'd either simply be landing the plane like a stud or he'd be yelling, "BRACE BRACE BRACE BRACE!" In that case, we were to assume crash position – heads between our knees kissing our ass goodbye. If that went well, he'd then be telling us to stay put or again he'd be yelling, but this time, "EVACUATE EVACUATE EVACUATE!"

This is where MacGyver steps in. He gives me the briefing on our tag team rescue effort where he rips off the door and I'm the first one out. I told him I liked the plan so far. Then, I was to escort everyone from the plane to safety. To be honest, I was amped about the idea. Don't get me wrong. I was scared of course. But feeling like I had a purpose or some control in what was going on was reassuring on some level. Maybe it kept me from tearing up like a little girl. Anyway, I had a heroic vision of busting through a ring of smoke from that plane with a baby in one arm and a little dog in the other while Chariots of Fire echoed in the background. Hell, I'd run in slow motion just for dramatic effect. I looked over to my left at the other exit. Two poor guys that didn't know each other just sitting there, eyes shut, head down, probably praying. I looked back at MacGyver, and honestly said, "That side of the plane is dead." Auh, I know. That's twisted, but I was using humor, however tasteless, to cope with the situation. Deal with it. It wasn't just me. MacGyver said "Yep," and we both smiled.

Fast forward 20 minutes and though it was a miserably crappy, weaving, rocking approach, the pilots landed the plane like silk on the runway to a waiting entourage of rescue vehicles that lined the runway pacing us in case of disaster. The pilot gets on the PA system all cocky and says, "I know that was scary for everyone, but now you know why they still have us up here and it's not all automated."

I share this story, because it's important for people to understand that shit hits the fan every now and again for all of us. This plane story is probably the coolest one I have thus far. It's better than the one time I got to see Tony Danza as a keynote speaker receiving an honorary diploma from my sister-in-law's University of Dubuque college graduation. Go Spartans. My coping mechanism with the plane was humor while others invoked prayer, tears or simply no response at all. You've all heard of people involved in near miss situations or dealing with tragic loss talking about living each day to the fullest because you never know when your last day will come. I don't think it's bad advice, but I don't think it's very realistic. I spent a decent amount of time watching the other passengers as the plane made its approach. For me, time slowed and I was more enthralled in people watching than the fact that we were in a serious situation. I'll bet more than one "promise to God" was made during that flight. I guess what I'm painfully trying to drag out of myself is that it didn't take this ordeal for me to know that I could get more out of life if I wanted to. It didn't take a plane scare to know that I needed to drop a few pounds and start exercising because I've been given a second chance. I didn't cheat death and now owe it to someone to go on a crusade as a motivational speaker. I went home, sat on the couch, and told the story to co-workers the next day. It's a pretty freakin' cool story. Then I ate unhealthy lunch, got indigestion, and dealt with it.

I will change when I'm ready to change and so will you. Adrenaline passes, and you clean the shit out of the fan and move on. When you want to make real changes, make them.

• 7 •

Dat Scwewy Wabbit

Frustration often rears its head from our interactions with others. I'll bet the majority of people have at least one co-worker that drives them up a wall from time to time for what amounts to a marginally insignificant reason. Whatever the case, you find yourself wanting to slap this person and they don't even know it. But some of you are saying right now, "Hey, I like all my co-workers. You're wrong on this one." You can see where I'm going with this - YOU'RE that person. I hate to break it to you. Take your damn tupperware home, clean out the coffee pot, stop stealing other people's staplers, and you'll be a better person. Otherwise, someone's going to go all Elmer Fudd and pull a shotgun on you.

My frustration with others usually stems from the social structure in which we live. Social classes often dictate behavior, and for many that means appearance and attitude, as well as and diction and delivery. Time for another short quiz guaranteed to flare up those frustration nerves.

1. You pass your company's sales guy in the aisle as he wanders around doing no real work whatsoever. You try to avoid eye contact, but he's got nothing better to do than bug you. You politely say, "Hello Steve." He hasn't bothered to ever learn your name, so he flashes that plastered fake smile and says, "Hey there:
    a. Chief
    b. Buddy
    c. Pal
    d. Bro (or Bra' if he thinks it's cooler)

2. You're waiting in line to order fast food, and the customer in front of you is going nuts because they asked for their cheeseburgers without ketchup, but the cheeseburgers have ketchup and the customer is having a heart attack

over the situation. The reason they feel as if they need to raise a public stink over the matter is because:

   a. They feel they are better than someone who works fast food, though their job isn't any better
   b. Despite their colossal order of super-sized everything, they are crabby due to them being on a diet (notice the super-size diet coke)
   c. The person behind the counter is just asking for it because they have piercings and tattoos and you know how "those people" are
   d. Their life sucks and they want to take it out on someone else

3. You're driving in heavy traffic, and you notice there is some jerk weaving in and out of traffic as if he's driving the #19 car sponsored by Black and Decker (or Craftsman or Home Depot or some other tool/hardware guys – shut up NASCAR fans. This is only an analogy. Quit freaking out because the #19 car is actually sponsored by Tide, but the driver is leaving the team at the end of the season to go drive for your arch rival's team…..blah blah blah). Where was I? Oh yeah, so anyway, this schmuck is getting nowhere fast but he's tailgating and breaking hard and bound to cause a ten-car pile-up in the next few minutes. But it's okay because there is actually a legit reason the person is driving like a lunatic. It's that:

   a. He is a lunatic
   b. She is texting her friend as she drives and who can be expected to text and drive safely at the same time?
   c. The person didn't realize there would be traffic up and down major roads at 8am on a Monday. Who could have predicted that?
   d. They drive a BMW. It's okay. (The judges also would have accepted Mercedes Benz, Lexus, or any car sounding Italian by name)

4. You are watching TV, and due to the 49 minutes of commercials per hour, you notice which of the following commercials that makes you so mad you want to slap a baby.

   a. A household product ad featuring a Beaver Cleaver

mom trying to do a hip-hop rap to look cool and stay in touch with today's youth. Notice the self-hug pose at the end with the Run DMC bling.

b. A perfume ad (you think) that throws seven random words at you coupled with obscure flashes of body parts best described as "maybe an elbow or armpit." Despite the attempts to reach a profound level, never once is the product name mentioned, pictured, or even hinted at. Add to this the fact that it's shown during NBC's laugh a lot primetime sitcom line-up, the commercial is likely being watched by those that do the bulk of their shopping at Walmart, not Nordstrom's.

c. Ads for upcoming reality show about someone who wouldn't be famous under any circumstance aside from the fact that is exactly why they are famous and therefore in need of a reality show that exploits their unfounded famousness……huh?

d. Car commercials that try to sell 15mpg in their new model "The Behemoth" as a step forward in gas reduction. I'll admit it's a small price to pay to have the seating for 8 that you'll never need, and 14, NOT 13, cup holders in each vehicle.

It's at this point somebody should just shoot me for noticing.

Author's Note: Upon editing, I read this sentence and had no idea what I originally meant or why this sentence ended up here. Apparently, I frustrate myself as well)

5. It's election time and you're trying to decide which candidate to vote for. The problem revolves around the fact that we are bred to hate and distrust most politicians, yet have allegiance to a political party based on one or two key areas that affect our lives. We are constantly in battle to find concrete reasons to support a candidate, but we also don't trust the media and their corporate owned agendas. Damn the man. How on earth are we to make an educated decision? Let me offer up four frustrating answers.

a. Stay unregistered and don't vote at all. Upset all the

people that go nuts when you don't vote. Let your voice be silent and enjoy the lack of jury duty the rest of the suckers have to serve. Just remember to shut the hell up about anything political since you didn't bother to exercise your given rights.
b. Vote on historical trends. If you're rich or old, you're republican. If you care about the environment or you are under the age of 30 but still living like a college student, vote democrat. Who cares about the real issues? Pick a political stereotype and stick with it.
c. You're a complete nut case and you don't mind throwing your vote away. Go ahead and vote for the independent candidate. Be proud of your 4% representation.
d. You live in Florida. Just punch holes all over the ballot. It won't matter. Your scanners are rigged anyway. Sit back and soak up the sun for now. The next president will find a way to tax it on you.

I am frustrated just writing about this stuff. And you know what they say - frustration leads to anger. Anger leads to hate. Hate leads to the dark side.

May the force be with you in these situations.

For others, frustration is commonly self-inflicted. We are not perfect. On special occasion, we have perfect moments. For example, this book is virtually perfect. I'm just kidding of course, but seriously it's perfect. While we aren't the perfect beings we might strive to be, we hold ourselves to difficult standards. Find a person that seems to have no cares in the world, and you'll find imperfections all over the place. The contentment stems from their acceptance of who they are. The person may be a tool or a deadbeat, but they obviously have figured one thing out. It doesn't pay to go through life beating yourself up like so many of us do.

My wife (let me start by saying that I am aware that starting any sentence with, "My wife," has the potential for devastatingly bad results and therefore I will be choosing my words wisely), bless her heart, beats herself up over the smallest things. This is a woman who has a wealth of knowledge, hobbies, and passion for life. She balances a great marriage, strong family bonds, and a committing social life, but if she misplaces a coupon, she wigs out and curses herself for being careless. Her frustration lies in the fact the she allows too little room for imperfection. I try to work with her in this, but for some reason when I say, "Baby. You're far from perfect. Don't worry about it," it doesn't seem to help. Don't shake your head at this book. I was just kidding. She's perfect to me. Are those the magic words you wanted to hear? There you go.

Many of us set expectations so high that we're bound to fail. I go through just about every day trying to be a better person, maybe not consciously, but kinda sorta in general. I take blame for things that go wrong because I do not believe in passing the buck, but I know that I am better served for learning from mistakes than kicking myself because they happened. I am not afraid (often) to make mistakes, nor do I stress and get frustrated at the mistakes more than usually necessary. Dwelling on the problems feeds the frustration and stress. Nobody needs that. The energy would be much better used trying to improve the situation, fix the problem, or tuck away a bit of experience for a wiser tomorrow.

Wherever the sources of your daily frustration stem from, keep them in check as best you can. Accept the fact that we all drive each other nuts with our habits and behaviors from time to time.

• 8 •

__Counting to Ten__

It's the first way you see people trying to cope with anger and frustration (at least on TV). It's always a male, usually cartoon-like, with steam coming from his ears with the sound of whistles blowing. He has to count to ten to calm the rage within, lest he become homicidal in the coming moments. I believe with great confidence that this has never worked in a real-life scenario. Should anyone actually try, I think it would go something like this.

Angry Man: *Hhrrr hrr rrrrrrrr....Aaaaggghh*

Pleading woman (aka: voice of reason): *Now Hank. Just calm down now. Take it easy. Just take it easy and count to ten.*

Angry Hank (yes, he suddenly gets a name): *Hrrh ummph..... One........... two...... Oh F*ck this! I'm outta here.*

Beep....Beep.....Beep.......This was a test of the emergency anger response system. Had this been a real emergency, what you've just read would have been followed by instructions. This was only a test.

This concludes our test of the emergency anger response system. We now return you to your regularly scheduled reading.

Part Three

Finding the Humor in Life

• 9 •

Humor in Strange Places

I took a shower today while wearing one sock. I'd be happy to explain why if you care to read about it. I spent the day wearing two socks as most people would, but it wasn't until I got home that I noticed I had a large piece of duct tape stuck to the bottom of one sock. I tried to pull it off, but it ruined the sock. I wasn't too upset as it was an old sock, and the other sock I was wearing wasn't its match anyway (that's just how I roll). So I threw the ruined sock away and spent much of the rest of the quiet evening at home wearing just the one sock. That is odd for some, I realize. For me it wasn't so much odd as it was just a Friday. Later, I went to take a shower, and after stripping down to everything but that one lone sock, I thought about stepping into the shower still wearing it. I thought, what would it mean to wear one sock into the shower?

I freely admit that I have forgotten to take clothes off before stepping into the shower. I don't mean I've walked in there fully dressed (unless I was drunk), but I have on occasion forgotten the socks or underwear. I've also been close to leaving a shirt on from time to time. But I protest that my absent-minded tendencies are far different from this situation. I thought about purposely leaving the sock on, if nothing else just to see how strange it may feel.

So, in I go to the shower and just before I turn it on, I look around as if there is a camera watching me. It truly feels weird how certain aspects of behavior are hard-wired into the brain. Turning the shower on, I felt as if I was breaking some rule by wearing the sock. As it got soaked, I tried not to think about how ridiculous the situation was. I tried to just go about my business, washing my hair, etc, but I couldn't help but think about my right foot. Certainly, it felt a bit heavier, almost like wearing a cast. But thoughts started to swirl in my head. Does anybody (reasonably sane) do this? Does it make me strange or curious? If I then write about it, as I am now, will that freak anyone out? What will my parents think if they read it? By most accounts, I'm pretty normal. Maybe quirky, but mostly normal. Does a small act like this pole vault me into a different class? What does it mean to be eccentric?

Then my wife came and peaked in on me. You'd think I'd been caught doing something else. I had no real explanation. She shrugged her shoulders at me as if to say, "Well. I'm not surprised. You have a little bit of idiot in you after all." She does take responsibility in choosing to spend her life with me. I didn't hide this behavior when we were dating years ago. I would have if I'd been smart enough to get away with it. But alas, I'm not that bright. There I stood, with soap in my eyes, wearing one sock, running out of hot water while my wife stood there letting the cold air in the bathroom and shaking her head with a sort of pitiful look. She said to me, "You know that's my sock you're wearing?"

__Author's Note:__ I have dropped this little anecdote in social conversation numerous times. Most recently, somebody misheard the context and somehow thought I was eating a Big Mac in the shower. Turns out, eating a Big Mac is very messy in the shower and shredded lettuce is a bit of a pain to scoop up around the drain. Who would have thunk it?

Life comes at us with humorous situations every day. Comedians make their living helping point that out to us. We pay them (sometimes very very well) for that gift. Laughter is the great equalizer. I like to take stock of the little things each day that make me chuckle – like the word "chuckle." I think for me it's other people that make me laugh the most. Now it's easy to watch people and pick on them for the way they behave, what they wear, or how they look. That's not nearly the same as appreciating the humor contained within. If you laugh at someone because they are short or overweight or have a disability, someone should have not only the right, but the obligation to slap you. That's not funny. What would be funny is watching you get slapped. That would be downright hysterical. Funny is a guy wearing shorts with black socks and sandals. Funny is someone trying to push open a door that says "Pull." Funny is someone that slips on an icy sidewalk but doesn't fall but does that weird catch your balance gyration almost break your hip arms flailing dance. That's funny. LAUGH AT IT!!! It's okay.

Another thing that you need to remember is that people are laughing at you too. Don't tell me you haven't looked back at old photos to the styles of hair and clothes and thought the photos should be sealed in an envelope and burned immediately. What you probably didn't realize is that while you were cool at the time, because "everyone was doing it," there was somebody out there laughing their ass off when you walked by them. What goes around, comes around. Laugh it up and enjoy the next trend. Personally, I'm waiting for Cross Colours to come back into fashion, maybe get myself a De La Soul hat.

I'm pretty sure that people are laughing at me each day. I'm well aware that I get caught mumbling to myself. Heck, I bet I get caught arguing with myself. What I don't know is all the other goofy stuff that may make people laugh at me behind my back. Maybe I've got quirks I have yet to identify. If so, people have most certainly noticed, but I would prefer at this point that they just keep it to themselves. My fragile ego cannot handle the abuse. Chances are that you have some of these same quirks. I cannot say for certain, but I know I've laughed at plenty of you. Just the other day, I watched a woman try to

---

Author's Note: *My wife was proof reading this chapter and discovered that there was no end to this sentence. It ended with "woman try to" and that was it. I apparently just moved on to the next paragraph. I have no idea what I was supposed to type there, so I leave it in as Exhibit A, your Honor. The author clearly demonstrates his ADD and fact that he's a moron for leaving the evidence for all to see.)*

Communication is another source of endless humor. If you don't believe me, sit a five-year-old in front of you and discuss global politics. I bet you it will be the best political discussion you've ever had. And you'll be voting for Sponge Bob for president next term as well. I think everyone should try and debate a small child on any subject whether it's how long a game of peek-a-boo could last, or which Pokémon character possesses the most mettle. If you have a child nearby, I implore you to try this experiment. If the kid doesn't suspect that you are up to something that may result in a time-out or early bedtime, they just might cooperate.

Questions to ask kids between the ages of 4-6:

1. If you could be any animal, what would it be and why?
2. How is your favorite TV show reflective of today's social issues?
3. Where's your butt and what noises does it make?
4. What have you done this year to justify Santa's return visit to your home?
5. How do you think we can resolve the unrest in the Middle East?

Assuming you were able to pry them away from the television and get them to answer these questions, my guess is that you have as much insight into the world as one day will allow. And I'm guessing it was damn funny as well. If you aren't smiling at the end of the questions, you've just interviewed Damien. May God have mercy on your soul.

Random thought alert!!!

The male peacock: To lure the female, the male displays his impressive plumage. Do you know why? Cuz if his name means anything at all, he needs something else to show off.

While we're on random humorous thoughts, let me tell you about an amusing moment I had today. While I sit here typing this, I am enjoying the company of my little cat, Skeeter, quietly curled up on my lap. She is reluctantly giving affection these last couple days as a result of a vet visit to pull a tooth. The vet put her under for the procedure and the anesthetic sometimes leaves kitties a bit constipated. I know this is wonderful knowledge for you, but if you stay with me a couple more sentences, I'll explain. So I visited the vet for some laxative medicine to get the bowel movements going again for my dear kitty, and afterwards I stopped by the grocery store to pick up a couple items my wife had asked me to grab. On my way out, daily trivial thoughts floated around in my head. Nothing out of the ordinary, you see.

It's just all about timing.....timing, and a filter that sometimes doesn't keep our outer voice quiet at appropriate moments. There were a couple of supermarket employees just outside the door taking a smoke break as well as several people making their way to the entrance as I exited. I've got both hands clamped down on the shopping cart as I push aggressively through the automatic doors. As is human nature, I made eye contact with a couple of the people walking by. What came out of my mouth was, "Kitty's gonna poo tonight."

I have no explanation for why I said it aloud. In fact, it took me a moment to realize that one singular thought had indeed escaped my lips. What's worse is that I'd said it with great enthusiasm and a little stank on it. Like, "Hell ya. That's what's gonna happen. Yeah." Don't worry. I didn't scream it out or get in anyone's face. I'm not a lunatic. Yet those poor shoppers and grocery employees were left with an awkward moment that likely stayed with them for a few minutes afterward. As I quietly walked to my car, I shook my head, which probably added to strangeness of my behavior. It probably looked like I was talking to myself, which was kind of what I was doing.

As I drove home, I chuckled to myself knowing this was exactly the type of spontaneous moment that makes life fun. I'm not immune to embarrassment by any stretch, but I'm quick to usually dismiss it once I've got perspective of the moment. Today's little exchange was as funny to me as it gets. My only wish would be to know what thoughts ran through those people's heads. There's no embarrassment there. I challenge each of you have the same moment from time to time. Now I know it may lose some of the spontaneity, but I can suggest a couple scenarios that will leave you chuckling while others are scratching their head.

1. Car Wash – make sure you visit a car wash with guys that do the finish wipe down and vacuum, etc. while you wait outside the car. After tipping them nicely and thanking them for their service, get in your car, start to drive away, stop suddenly, get out of your car (completely) and go up to the guy and ask quietly (almost in a whisper), but seriously, "You didn't look in the trunk, did you." When he responds, "no" just walk away slowly. If he's still

looking as you drive away, put a finger to your lips in a little ssshhhhhhhh moment. You may not want to visit that car wash again for a year or so.

2. Elevators – This one is fun, and I can tell you from personal experience that it is a very weird situation for everyone involved. Making sure you are one of the last people to step on to the elevator, continue to face forward into the elevator even though everyone else turns around to face the door. Make sure your riding all the way down. Should anyone get off on a floor before you, wish them a good day and thank them for riding the elevator with you. If the elevator stops on the way down and more people get in, continue to face your direction with the conviction that only a psycho can possess.

3. Stand outside a shopping mall right at the curbside facing the front of the mall on a busy day. If you can pick a relatively sunny day, it makes it more fun. As people get near the curb walking from the parking lot, look up to the sky as if the most interesting thing is happening. This is a "made you look" moment. Within a minute or so, you'll get a taker who will glance up to see what's so interesting. The real fun is that this is about the time they need to be watching where they walk because of the curb. Oh, I've done this. And yes, people do trip on the curb. I'm not proud of it. I may even be getting a one-way ticket south in the afterlife for it, but I admit it might be the hardest thing not to laugh when someone eats it tripping on the curb to stare at your nothingness in the sky. It's very twisted and cruel, but very funny. It's truly a fine line to walk. If you want to tone down the likelihood of people falling, try this inside the mall. Grab a few friends to help you with this one. One person looks up focusing intensely on some spot while your friends, coming from different directions and seeming unrelated, notice your staring and look up for themselves. All activity stops as masses of people follow suit not wanting to be left out of the commotion. Take the time to maybe point and whisper to a friend near you as if there is more to the situation.

Social experiments are fun.

• 10 •

I Cannot Believe I Laughed at That

Humor allows us to push away stress and, in my not too humble opinion, forms the backbone of happiness. But humor and laughter can be tricky, misunderstood, or flat out inappropriate in some scenarios. For example, I laugh at my wife every day. I also laugh with my wife every day. I'm well aware that one of those two sentences sound like trouble. But it's sooooooo true. I cannot help it, nor do I want to help it. She has given her blessing on this book, and so I call her free game. My wife says the silliest stuff from time to time. Unfortunately for her, I get the greatest pleasure when people's brains malfunction, so she puts up with my laughter. Most of the time she is cool with it, because she has an amazing sense of humor herself and rarely takes herself too seriously. There are occasions that it may seem as if I am picking on her and nobody likes to feel like they're an idiot or have somebody laugh at their expense. I must be sensitive to her feelings of course. I mean I keep laughing, but I give her a hug as well. Then I have to sleep in the spare room. At least it's not on the couch. I don't have it all figured out yet. Here's a couple more little tidbits for you to gnaw on.

I have a friend that works for an organization called Feed My Starving Children (FMSC). If you haven't heard of it, please check it out. This organization in a nutshell does its best to raise awareness while packaging food that is sent directly to starving children throughout the world. It is comprised of dedicated individuals and volunteer help that work daily to combat starvation in areas of need. Now, unlike many of us to whom a job is a job, my friend has a deeper commitment to her work. However, like most of us, she gets tired at the end of the day. One evening as she came to work at her secondary job, I jokingly asked her, "How are the all the starving children doing today." Without missing a beat, she replied, "Still starving." And with this we had a little laugh. I told her she was going to hell for laughing at the poor innocent helpless starving children. But what can you do? It was a time for humor. She'd had a long day at a draining job only to have to come work another job. If you let the weight of the world lay on your shoulders without blowing off steam every now and again, you'll truly collapse. Life will sap your energy, your creativity, and your happiness. That's my thought anyway. Of course, my friend was not "laughing" at starving children. She needs what everyone needs – a break. And people need other people to help us with that. I've volunteered my time twice at Feed My Starving Children facilities. That number should be a whole lot higher, but we cannot fight every battle or give to all causes. We pick the ones that tug greatest to our heartstrings and give what we can. I believe that's all that can be realistically asked of us. All of us can give more. You could've taken the money you spent on this stupid book and given it to a charity or used the time you've spent reading this dribble to help an organization such as FMSC. But I guess what I'm saying is that we are all allowed to laugh at the starving children from time to time. Metaphorically speaking of course. Damn, you're going to hell too for even smiling at that.

Author's Note: My friend no longer works for FMSC. But yes, the children are still starving. *Insert Sad Trombone sound….. wah wah

I lost my grandfather a few years back. He spent much of the last couple years of his life struggling against several ailments. He body was slowly breaking down, and he spent much of the time on bed rest towards the end. Though his passing saddened me, I was relieved that he wouldn't have to suffer each day. I have fond memories of him from my childhood and it was tough to see him unable to function with the livelihood he enjoyed. My grandmother and aunt put together a collage of pictures for the service, which allowed us to grieve and yet celebrate my grandfather at the same time. Now I'm not about to write a whole blurb about it being okay to laugh at a funeral because you told a story about the person you lost and everybody laughed and cried, etc. That should be a given. Personally, my funeral better be a party. And I want the volume uncomfortably loud. I'll take it a step further. I'd like to award a prize to the person who recites the funniest story they know about me to those at the funeral. I want people's bellies to hurt from laughter (in between the inconsolable tears from my departure of course). But I digress. This story of my grandfather goes deeper.

My sister has three children, ages 10, 8, and 2 at the time of the funeral. The two older children understood to a degree that their great grandfather had died, but a funeral is sometimes a difficult place to be with children. The youngest, my little niece, obviously had no concept of the occasion and though nobody would hold that against her, my sister was concerned that she would be a distraction at the service. As many funeral homes have, there is a lower level convenient for these situations. They had some kid's videos and games, stuff to keep them entertained if not distracted. After the service, we were going to head over to the grandparent's home to spend some time as a family. My sister and I were cleaning up in the lower area from the coffee cake and drinks that were put out when she burst into tears in front of me. Because grief strikes people differently, I didn't know if this was just one of the emotional waves that had hit her. She looked at me through tears, yet her expression puzzled me. I asked her what was wrong. She explained that she was thinking about taking the kids home and skipping the visit to my grandparent's house. She was about to say that she was worried that her youngest daughter would be too loud and would wake my grandfather who would likely be laying down resting at the house. Sitting there at his funeral, this was the thought that ran through her head. She was so conditioned that the thought came into her head (and almost out her mouth) before she realized it. She was in tears with guilt for the thoughts and even more guilt for the humor with which it possessed. I love my sister very much, and I had to let her know there was nothing wrong with laughing at the situation. I believe it was one of the more genuinely funny moments I've experienced. I miss my grandfather. I believe he would have laughed as well.

Let's lighten the mood a bit, shall we? How about a little mad lib? Feel free to write directly into the book or photocopy the page to use it multiple times. Here it goes. I'll be using an excerpt from Redd Foxx's unauthorized ghost-written autobiography entitled, *Elizabeth – I'm coming…but don't wait up.*

In every man's _____(noun), there comes a time when he has to make _____ (pl noun). I didn't want to be embarrassed, so I _____(verb) for nearly _____ (number) hours before I decided to _____(verb). I mean, seriously what kind of animal would want me to throw a _____(adj)_____(noun) to prove I had the libido of a _____(animal)? Holy _____(exclamation)! It's not as if I _____(verb) to _____(place).

At _____ (time of day), I called my buddy _____ (famous person). As it turns out, he was watching _____ (TV show) already, and he had seen the footage where I _____ (verb) with no regard for the safety of myself or my _____ (pl noun). I thought my days as a comedian were over. _____(exclamation). I couldn't book a gig in _____(city). I'll bet there aren't more than _____(number) people in this world that know that type of pain. That's what it was like to be a _____ (adj) man during the _____ (period in history).

• 11 •

Thank You, Drive Through

I'm talking to my friend one day and he tells me he went to his bank to deposit a check. Now he's been at the same bank for a while and there just happens to be this little cutie that works the drive-up. He deposits his check, getting $20 back in cash so he can fill his tank that day. As most guys would admit, it's always a good day when you are waited on by an attractive woman. So naturally, he's enjoying what would otherwise be a routine, if not boring, experience. The deposit pod shoots down through the tube and when he opens the pod, $300 is in the envelope. Astonished, he looks up towards the cute teller and she smiles to him. He does a double take and looks again. She's still smiling and though a bit confused by his good fortune, he takes off.

Ladies, I want to explain something. This IS how our brain works. We see a cute girl smile at us, and we do dumb stuff like think that maybe they're just giving us $300 for no good reason. As it turns out, my buddy filled out the deposit ticket backwards, asking for $20 to go into his account and $300 in cash back to him. Of course, there's more. In his haste, he also drove away with the deposit tube. A couple minutes later, he's pulling back into the drive-up with smile that says, "Yes. I'm all sorts of stupid." As he replaces the deposit tube, the teller is still smiling.

Because I freely admit that I'm no better, let me share a tidbit of idiocy. I eat too much fast food. I regularly stop for breakfast, even after vowing for the umpteenth time that I will no longer fill my body with McDonald's and Burger King. Alas, I pulled into the Burger King, ordered a breakfast burrito, cheesy tots, and Dr. Pepper. I pulled to the second window, greeted the less than enthusiastic drive through attendant, and paid for my meal; truly another $4.08 well spent. I handed him a $20-dollar bill, received my change, and drove away. I know you've already seen the punch line here coming, but it took me a couple miles before

I figured out that I didn't wait around for the food. The worst part is that I know I'm going back there again tomorrow or the next day, and they might remember me as the guy who just likes to drive away after paying. Actually, that's not the worst part. The worst is that it isn't the first time I've done this. It's probably the fifth or sixth time it's happened. I have problems. I wonder who eats my food when I leave it behind?

I have another friend with whom I haven't talked in some time. We lost touch as people do and realistically, I doubt we'll keep in touch. That part of life is unfortunate. It would be nice to have the time to stay close with everyone you meet. But I doubt I will forget some of his stories. He has a thirst for life that few can parallel. He's a doctor that spent part of his schooling and residency in the western parts of Illinois, home of plush farm land and small towns. Between residency and the brief breaks to try and put together any semblance of a social life, he would make the journey from western Illinois back to the Chicagoland area to hang out with friends. At that time, he rode a large crotch rocket of a motorcycle, ripping across the quiet farm country at 100mph or more. He also rode his motorcycle well into the fall and he'd invested in clothing to keep him warm for the otherwise frigid drive. So on a particularly cold autumn day, he was on his way back from Chicago to Galesburg, about a 4-hour journey, when he had the need to pee.

Dressed in heavy black leather pants with under layers for warmth, decked out in an oversized black leather coat and jet-black helmet with tinted face shield, he looked like Darth Vader powering along the highway. As the urgency to pee escalated, he gunned the motorcycle to well over 120mph, desperate to get home quickly, not wanting to stop and strip through the layers of clothes just to relieve himself. When it became clear he might not be able to hold it, he noticed a highway rest area approaching. Pulling into the rest area at around 75mph, he came to screeching halt, threw the bike to the ground, and sprinted to the washroom. Without so much as removing his helmet, he clawed at the zipper and was barely able to get it down before going all over himself. Moments later, he realized that he wasn't alone in the restroom. A poor old man had been using the urinal across the bathroom and was no doubt alarmed as Darth Vader came bursting through the door sprinting to pee. He told me that he turned to see a frightened look on the man's face. A few seconds later as more travelers came to use the washroom, they greeted him with similar looks of confusion. After a minute or so he stood there alone in the bathroom still out of breath from sprinting to the restroom in a race against bladder control. Relieved in both mind and body, he looked up and saw the ridiculousness of the situation. In the mirror directly in front of him stood this leather clad goofball complete with monster helmet. He couldn't help but laugh at himself for a moment.

Now the story could end there, and the anecdote would already be mildly amusing, but oh no. That's not all. Ever have those moments where you know something is amiss, but you can't quite put your finger on it? Well, here's a guy that is staring at himself in the mirror and yet something isn't quite right. He finally realizes that there aren't mirrors in front of men's urinals. He's been pissing in the sink. How I wish I was there.

Author's Note: *No transition here whatsoever. It's a thing.*

I grew up playing baseball. My friends and I would play two versus two games, complete with invisible runners and right field outs and all the modifications necessary to enjoy four-man baseball. I'm not a bright man – did I mention that already? So during one of these games, I had the brilliant idea to try and make the bat collide with the ball while my buddy threw the ball back to the pitcher after he'd thrown a pitch way outside and we had to chase it down about twenty feet away. As he chucks the ball past me back to the pitcher, I whip this aluminum bat straight up in the air end over end. I look up and all I see is the midday sun baking down on us. Of course, the bat comes down and just cracks me in the forehead, rattling my brain like never before. I'm knocked into a whole new world of stupid. It takes a minute for me to come to my senses but probably out of sheer embarrassment, I continue playing. We finish our half of the inning, take the field, and after a quick 3 up and 3 down, we are again up to bat. I'm sweating heavy in the summer heat and I take a second to wipe the perspiration from across my brow. My buddy points at my hand and all he can mutter is a scared, "Dude. You're bleeding." It was a bit of an understatement. My hand was covered with blood. I took off my baseball cap and the inside brim was soaked red.

I lived about 100 yards from where we were playing baseball. But as every boy knows growing up, most injuries we sustain do not draw sympathy from parents but rather anger. It isn't that parents are mean or uncaring. We just do dumb shit to get ourselves hurt. So very quickly you must decide if the reason you got hurt was justifiable. Often, you'd do your best to try to hide it to avoid any trouble. Mom doesn't mind if you accidentally cut you finger with a knife making a sandwich. Mom's a bit pissed if that same injury comes from you learning to juggle with knives. You get the point. So instead of coming home, I ran with my friend in the opposite direction to his house and called my mom to explain how I'd split my forehead open and somehow had failed to notice for a half hour. She was less than amused and was waiting on the front porch when I came running home. If you haven't seen a head wound, they always look worse than they are. When I pulled my cap off to show my mother, she was horrified by the amount of blood. As it turns out, it only needed about eight stitches to close a small one-inch gash. Here's the kicker – though my mother loves me dearly and was concerned for my well-being, I remember how upset she was that I ruined one of our washcloths with my bloody head.

The truth is that we all do wonderfully dumb dumb dumb stuff that makes for great stories, amusing memories, necessary learning experiences, and even entertaining reading from time to time. I have many more of these stories, but I'll hold back for now. I still have a few pages I might need to fill at the end of the book. So for now, this chapter was simply included for comic relief. Thank you, drive through.

• 12 •

Bring on Bizarre Thoughts

I know it isn't just me, but I times I wonder how strange my thoughts are. I think for many, the line of bizarre thinking stems from our dreams. I'd like to dedicate an entire section of this book to dreams, but as you can tell by now, I don't really know that much about…..well….anything. So, let's make it up for a moment. It isn't as if this book is dripping with integrity. We'll split bizarre thoughts into two categories: Thoughts we have while awake and thoughts that spring forth from sleepy dreams.

Category One: My eyes were open when this popped into my head

<u>Thought #1</u>

Your own death – I cannot find anybody that hasn't fantasized about their own demise. Regardless of why death knocks on your doorstep, chances are you've thought about your own death. More so than that, I'll bet you've thought about your own funeral. In most cases you've died relatively young, and you're thinking about how choked up everyone would be. You think, "Who'd show up at my funeral and be balling their eyes out." Ten dollars says the following people were in your thoughts. First off, your family of course would be there. But I bet you pictured an ex-boyfriend/girlfriend showing up out of nowhere grief stricken by your loss and the guilt they feel for letting you go or screwing up the relationship in the first place. And in this fantasy death thought, you're happy that they're all upset. You're so twisted. I think you need counseling. Co-workers or classmates show up as well. Your funeral is always well attended in your mind. Here's where it all gets a little disturbing. There is always one person in these thoughts that either doesn't show up to the funeral or doesn't feel any loss at your departure. And even though this is your own brainscreen, you hold it against the person IN REAL LIFE! How incredibly messed up is that?

Thought #2

Super powers – Everyone wants super powers. If someone says they don't want super powers, stab them. They will bleed because they don't have super powers.

What kind of super powers would you want? You want to fly or have super human strength. You want to be Wolverine and be bad-ass plus heal quickly? How about invisibility? (By the way, EVERY guy has wanted invisibility powers to gain access to changing rooms, locker rooms, bedrooms, etc. It's just the way we are, and we are simple creatures. I cannot stress this enough. Sorry ladies, it's true.) What I'm trying to find are the goofy powers that each of us has wanted at some time or another. Have you ever wanted the ability to jump off tall buildings and splat into the pavement like a cartoon character, peel your flat-self up, and shake yourself back to regular shape? How cool would it be to have the ability to drive a car like the Flintstones? 50 mph with your feet would be sweet. No gas – no problem. I want you to search for that special power that sets you apart from the norm. Yes, being able to fly or read minds would be handy, but what if your hands had the ability to turn into any kitchen utensil like fork or spoon or spatula. That would damn handy. Ha, that's punny.

Thought #3

Getting away with murder – I'll bet that most of have thought at one time or another, "What if I pushed him/her?" Now before I get framed for premeditated murder, I want to express that this thought comes for no apparent reason to us around people with whom we actually like. That's the twisted part. You know you've been hanging out with someone, looking over a balcony and thought, "I could get away with it." Sick puppies. You should be locked away now. But who hasn't watched too many CSI or Law and Order shows and thought they could plan the perfect crime? Personally, I feel murder is overrated. I think we should start a victimless crime spree. Who can be the most notorious J-walker? Did you hear about that guy who broke into houses cutting the warning tags off of mattresses and then went running with the scissors in his hands? That's the kind of stuff I want to hear about. Unless you're throwing momma from the train, you need to leave the murder thoughts to someone else.

Thought #4

Last person on earth - Let's assume for a moment that you are indeed the last person on earth (or one of the last people). This is a good thought to ponder while riding the train to work or while sitting at your desk zoning out when you should be working on the DPS report. Because in our thoughts we are never left in a post-apocalyptic, burned out, nuclear wasteland, let's just assumed that the world is in pretty good shape but everyone just sort of vanished. Isn't that usually how we picture it? It's so tough – do you loot stores for food and supplies, or do you explore all the areas that maybe you wouldn't normally have access to? I personally would take the time to break and blow stuff up. It would certainly be fun, yet anticlimactic without having someone to share it with. Oh well. It's better than pondering the "alone on an island with only one movie to watch" crap.

Before we move forward toward dreamy thoughts, let's ponder a few thoughts that may pop into our heads. Circle all that you've had in the last year or so. Keep in mind that if you circle more than 13 of these, you probably need help. Stop talking to yourself and call a shrink.

Did I leave the oven on?
Why are my socks yelling at me?
I look good in plaid
The number eight looks weird
I wish I had a pet monkey
Sometimes I'm scared to fart
How cool would it be to have six arms?
I like cheese….a lot
My cat watches me when I sleep
I want to bottle my burps
It's time we bring back pantomime
I wish my toes were self-cleaning
Good toast cannot be overrated
My butt jiggles even when I stop moving
I've never wanted to read binary
I want a wall of Velcro to jump on
Why do I wake up without pants so much?
Cows are harrier than I first thought
All robots smell like my grandmother
Do we really need the letter "K"?
Ever want to fill in your belly button?

I've always wanted to be a scarecrow
Bill Idol's cooler than people think
Long division was invented by Nazi's
Sometimes my knees move on their own
My car has multiple personalities
I want a dog that can drive a car
If you stab a clock, is it killing time?
I should shower with the lights off
Optimism is what it's cracked up to be
I want to connect a leopard's spots
Poetry should always rhyme
Bunk beds are never a good idea
I'd look thinner without hair
I'd look fatter without hair
My mother ruined my life
I ruined my mother's life
I'd like to roll down stairs in bubble wrap
Why don't we hug our dentists?
If you tickle me too much, I pee
Cocktail was a dumb dumb movie
Who still buys RC Cola?

Does red mean love or danger?	How is Bobby short for Robert?
Mister Rodgers was creepy but cool	My cock should glow in the dark
I need a job in a circus	I wear my sunglasses at night, too
Juggling is a useless talent	It's a good thing sharks don't have legs
When was the last time I skipped around?	I need to keep my lizard fat
Sometimes I cry at reality TV	I dance like a white guy should
I hate clowns	My significant other deserves a better title
I'm in love with a clown	The mullet should be embraced
My mother was a clown	"Brittany" is never an accountant
Pigtails are for the under 30 crowd	Hockey should be played by midgets
Spandex should only be made in small	Why can't cows walk downstairs?
I pop Advil like Jelly Beans	A sleepover is better than a hangover
I need to compliment people more	I'm tempted to stick my tongue in the fan
I need to just punch somebody today	Thank god permanent markers aren't
I like to watch people trip (and fall)	Buying a conversion van makes you creepy

Okay, how did you do? I assume that other random thoughts popped in your head while reading that list. Take the time to start your own list, but make sure you write the details down as well. After a couple months, go back and read the list. You'll likely be quite disturbed at the crazy thoughts that entered your head. But that's okay. You should be disturbed. You're a freak and should be locked away. Hurry, eat the list. That way people won't know and later they can say, "Oh yeah. She seemed like such a nice person. Never would have suspected she could do that." Let's move forward.

Dreams. Where to start? I was lying in bed the other night when suddenly somebody was knocking on the front door. I got up and starting walking when a realized I was wearing wooden Dutch clogs on my feet. *Clackity clack clack clackity stomp clack stomp.* As I made my way through the kitchen, I stopped to grab a ladle and a spatula, but my spatula wasn't in the drawer. I open the lower cupboard and there was a mini rhino, about 12 inches tall, guarding it. I pulled a mini-rhino treat out of my pocket, and thanked him for taking good care of my kitchen utensils. A few paces later, I was at the front door, but it wasn't a front door anymore. It was a life raft. With the strength of an adolescent bobcat, I hurled the raft through the air approximately 3 feet. Needless to say (but I'll do it anyway), I had no choice but to pile into a small VW Beetle with 27 clowns for a trip to McDonalds. And believe me when I tell you they gave Ronald a beating he is not likely soon to forget. This all takes place in Egypt of course with the Great Pyramid in the background. Vendors all lined up selling shirts that read "Ronald had it coming" and

"Clowns unite against the 'man'" and "My unconsciousness got to go to this cool dream and all I got was this crummy t-shirt." Somebody tries to hand me a glass of water, but I spilled it all over myself, and that's when I woke up. I'm not saying I wet the bed. I'm just saying it happens.

I assume you've had the same dream? But, what does it mean? If you own a dream analysis book, please burn it. They are often unnecessarily vague with their descriptions and all too quick to rush to judgment in their interpretations of your dreams. Dream interpretation is difficult and a false read on a dream can lead to a life a crime. It's totally true. I saw a Dateline story on it. Trust me, totally serious. As it happens, I am completely qualified to interpret your dreams. That is fortunate for the purposes of this book. Let me now dazzle you with some basics to dreams.

Any time there is water in your dream, perhaps a waterfall or the ocean, or you're playing in a pool, what that means it that you are simply thirsty. That fact that you wake up needing to pee each time is a secondary response. You may think it is metaphoric for something else, but alas it is not. Water = thirst. It's quite logical if you think about it. Say for example you dream about the outdoors with green pastures and meadows and flower fields. It's really a manifestation of your insecurities with money and the yearning for childhood where the cares were minimal. If you dream about cows, it usually means you wish to visit Rome. Maybe you didn't think you wanted to visit Rome, but you do. If you dream about co-workers, chances are that you don't like fish. I'm not making this up. Your dream book would have told you so, but now that you've burned it at my suggestion, you'll have to take my word for it.

Dude, check this out. Why don't your feet talk? That would be the best. Holy shit. What if your feet just talked to you, but the voice didn't match what you thought it would be? So like my toes have the voice of Morgan Freeman and they're all like, "Andy Dufresne, crawled through a river of….." and I'm like, "Shut up about it already. I get it. He's redeemed. Cue inspirational music and happy ending for the guy who got banged in prison but got out after twenty years to go live on a crappy boat."

Since we're sharing, that's one of my favorite movies.

But what if your toes didn't have a cool voice? What if your feet were voiced by something that sounded more like Gilbert Gottfried? Holy cow. You'd put on some socks and your feet would utter in that loud discordant voice, "Oh my God! Geez, somebody tell me why this guy cannot just wear argyles. A priest, a rabbi, and a horse walk into a bar. The bartender looks at the pole shoved up the...." And that's when you hurry up and put on shoes to shut your toes up.

Maybe it's good our feet don't talk. Where was I?

***Author's Note:** My wife didn't like this section on feet. She told me it came out of nowhere and was quite confusing lumped within this section of dreams. I agree. She's very smart. Alas, I am not.*

Part Four

Love and Relationships

• 13 •

1-800-Dial-a-friend

How many friends do you have? How many are real friends? How many can you truly confide in? I think everyone needs a few true friends. Everyone needs a couple people that will slap them when they make poor decisions and have their back at the same time. We need pals that will give you the advice you need, not the advice you want. You need a friend that will have you laughing until you cannot breathe. Maybe you'll even pee your pants a little. And that friend won't mind. In fact, they may even pee their pants too. Yah gross, eh?

I'm lucky to have a couple of these buddies. I think it's easier for guys. We require virtually no maintenance whatsoever. We all have a standard three to five things that we do with each other whether it's sports, movies, video games, poker, etc. We rarely deviate from the core activities (Note: There are exceptions to this rule when involved in couples' outings. We may be forced to participate in activities outside of said designated hangout routine, but it's not our choice. It's the significant others' faults). Anyway, we like it that way. It's simple and for most of us, that's what we want. Ladies, don't screw with that. Ladies need a different type of friend. They need friends that are more well-rounded and care about the details because I've learned one thing in my years of marriage. The details count. Mark my words – there will be more on that in a later chapter.

So like I was saying, do you find yourself struggling to build those tight friendships? Since this is a self-help guide to living book thing, I must ask the big questions. If so, here's the solution. Set your standards lower. Our friends are rarely perfect. In fact, most of us have at least one friend that by and large, most people cannot stand. Oh yeah, if you're nodding your head in agreement, go ahead. It's true. In fact, if you're not agreeing with this, well shit. You're the friend. Many people don't like you. That's okay. It's not as if you didn't already kind of know it. Change if you want to, but you really don't have to.

It's about finding the best qualities in each other to the help build the friendships. If I think about it, it's not hard to find positive qualities in each of my close friends that I truly admire. I'm not talking about the superficial stuff either. I have a friend that is a tremendous athlete. He runs, he climbs, he does adventure races, bikes, canoes, everything. It's not so much that he has the talent and physical tools to pull this stuff off. It's all about the enjoyment he gets from it. He's not an adrenaline junkie. Not hardly. Hell, he's afraid of snakes and has a healthy controlled fear of heights even though he's an accomplished rock climber and mountaineer. Rather, the fact that he throws himself into these scenarios with the joy a little boy jumping into the ball pit for the first time at a McDonald's play land. Geronimo!!! I admire that fact that gear breaks every time he uses it. I'm talking about high-end quality gear. I'm talking expedition gear. He kills it. And the best part is that it's sometimes not his gear. My gear has seen premature retirement in his hands. He trashed a pair of best snowshoes on the market inside of a week to the level that the company rep was astounded by the carnage beat into them. I am left in awe of this. During an adventure race, a jelly fish took the time to introduce itself to my friend by swimming up his shorts and stinging him on the nuts. He called me to recount the details of the epic battle known now simply as "Day of the Jelly Nuts." Not that he enjoyed the experience, but it was part of the adventure. I admire this. It's great to have that bond with close friends. You want them around, even if it means occasional bodily harm or misadventure.

Take a few moments to identify these qualities in your closest friends. Friends of convenience or friends from common interest alone don't seem to hold those same qualities. Tell me I'm wrong. Just because you've been around the person since grade school, doesn't mean that you genuinely have the strongest bond. My closest friend (notice I will NEVER use the term BFF – less I be shot in the head instantly) went to high school with me, but we didn't even hang out until our senior year. And even then, it was through another group of friends that we hung out. Eventually, people moved in different directions of life, but he and I remained close friends. Our friendship blossomed as we found those lifelong bonds that only the closest friends have. I know, that sounds all Brokeback and everything. But if we can turn up the maturity level for a moment (I won't ask of this much), having a connection with close friends makes life a bit sweeter. I have this same connection with my wife, however, that relationship comes with other perks.

• 14 •

I'd Like to Take You Home Tonight

Dating is tricky. Let me lend some scientific advice to help both sexes along. Humans attract mates much the same way other animals do, yet we tend to ignore the signals because we feel a heightened sense of evolutionary prowess in this department. Nothing could be further from the truth. Both sexes emit pheromones in the pursuit of a mate. Women's pheromones help the male understand when the female is most fertile, and the male pheromones give the female the opportunity to browse for a worthy suitor. How does this actually work, you ask? Well, I'll explain, so just keep reading. First, the female chemicals can only be released when a woman is truly looking for a mate. To give off the proper scent, it usually takes tight fitting clothing or a very little clothing at all. Garments such as baggy sweatpants and loose-fitting shirts and sweaters prohibit the release of the pheromones keeping the scents withheld and should be avoided by a woman seeking a quality partner. Also, an overabundance of makeup or glitter may give false impression to the male as the scents mimic that of the mating pheromones, but do not indicate that a woman is indeed looking for a partner.

Males looking to find a mate also release their scent to a woman. In many other animals, this scent is accentuated with physical exertion (sweat), but not for humans. Though the visual senses of the female may find this appealing at times, the scents given off from these activities mask the intention of the male causing confusion or disinterest from a potential partner. The male is looking to release that perfect scent that tells the female that he is most worthy of her attention. The pheromone release, surprisingly enough, smells much like the paper currency we use today. Women seem attracted to this scent above all, and many a male suitor can lure a woman with this scent even if he lacks the physical characteristics to make him more appealing.

And then there are hormones. Quite different than pheromones, hormones regulate our sexual characteristics and help us exhibit certain behavioral and physical traits. Though men and women produce the same hormones, I'm pretty sure it's just the levels of the hormones that determine the sex of the person. DNA might have something to do with it. You know, XY vs. XX chromosomes and all that. But really, I think it comes down to hormones. For example, testosterone is produced in higher quantities for males and estrogen is found in higher quantities for females. It's very very true that if a male produces or is given higher doses of estrogen, he may grow sizeable breasts. What is less commonly known is that his penis may fall off and be replaced with a vagina. I swear I read that from a doctor's office waiting room pamphlet. It was called, "Hormones and You – A guide to keeping your penis for men."

Testosterone is equally powerful. For men, it helps us grow hair, deepen our voice, and in very large doses, creates Magnum P.I. For women, testosterone is only produced in levels that should allow a woman to change a tire without help or make a decision without waffling back and forth for an hour. Higher concentrations do not have the same physical side effects men face with estrogen but may cause women to take up competitive tennis or wear flannel. To regulate hormone levels, our body takes in outside stimuli and filters it through our brain. Our brain filters these signals and sends off messages called synapses throughout the body. Our body replies by releasing the correct amounts of hormonal chemicals throughout the bloodstream and the result is seen in our behavior or appearance. Would you like a "For example?" I thought you would.

Example: 10-year-old Tommy is walking to school with his friends. His trips on a small bump in the sidewalk and face-plants. His friends laugh because that what boys do in that situation. It's hardwired into our brains at birth, and of course, it's funny as shit. Even as Tommy is going down in pain, signals are sent to his brain telling him this is gonna suck big time. The brain can react in two ways. If the signal is sent to release estrogen, then Tommy's reaction is to cry in front of his friends while their laughter echoes in his ears. If the brain fires off the cue to release testosterone in that situation, then Tommy will get up and punch the closest guy to him in embarrassment. Should

Tommy hit the pavement so hard that his head rattles and the brain cannot send out the proper signals, Tommy probably needs medical attention and it really doesn't matter. Let's just wish him a speedy recovery.

That was Body Chemistry 101. It's scientific truth. You don't even need to check it out to verify. I'm sure of it. Sorry to backtrack all the way back to basic development, but it is imperative that you have a sound understanding of the human makeup as you move forward towards finding that special someone. The next section will continue with dating etiquette.

Throughout our teenage years, most of us fumble with dating to a degree that seems borderline comedic if not outright pathetic. I heard somebody say that they wish they could go back and hook up with their first partner again to show them how much better they've gotten in bed. I, on the other hand, do not recommend this train of thought. And since you're reading my self-help guide to living and not theirs, listen up as to why. The awkwardness and failure that we experience lends to our appreciation of the talents we later gather. Never forget that.

These days dating has avenues that were not present to us. Besides the fact that your friends are often eager to match you up with a co-worker always described as having a "nice personality," we now have internet dating options like never before. The accessibility to people has grown exponentially. Go ahead and post a profile up on a website. Remember to describe yourself as "outgoing" and "casual" at the same time. Post a flattering selfie and decide whether you want a quick hook-up or an actual date, but remember – there are lots of crazy people out there. It's likely you're one of them. Be patient, not desperate.

Other dating avenues haven't changed much. You can always go the old-fashioned route. No, I don't mean finding a nice, wholesome girl at church or a strip club. I mean at a bar or a club. If it's instant gratification and you have minimal standards, then you're bound to get lucky. If this is your route, then you need to be prepared. Gentlemen, you need to make sure you have cash, a high drinking tolerance, and the patience to listen to long conversation you shouldn't put more than 50 words into. And remember, you agree with every opinion she has. You need to act like whatever comes out of her mouth is poetic truth that has never been uttered more beautifully. The ladies know you're full of crap, or at least they should. It doesn't really matter. Those are the hoops you're going to need to jump through to get with her anyway. As far as ladies as concerned, to hook up at the club or bar for the evening, you need only a pulse. From there, your options are open.

First dates can be scary for both involved. You both know that you'd like it to work out, but it's likely that one of you isn't as psyched about the probability of it happening with this match-up. So, that means someone's already climbing uphill at the beginning of the date. Here are some do's and don'ts for the first date.

DO	DON'T
Compliment her on her looks	Mention she has a great rack
Open the doors for her	Talk about your ex for any reason
Tell her to take her time getting ready	Text them from across the table
Laugh at his dumb jokes	Ask them if they're into S&M
Ignore one or two or his ignorant comments	Talk politics
	Use the word "Dude"
Accept that he'll sneak a peek at your breasts	Take them to a Jack Black movie
	Talk to him about marriage
Talk to her face, not her chest	Bring your children
Find interesting conversation to keep the date moving	Wear anything that makes a fashion statement
Use protection	Tell her about your alien abduction
Buy popcorn and candy at the movie	Mention you are co-dependent
Bathe and shave before the date	Offer her money for "special treatment"
Avoid using your cell phone the WHOLE date	
Keep the focus on them	

Keep to these simple rules and you're sure to have a great first date. Conversation should be held to simple topics. Use such starter questions as, "Tell me a little about what you do." Feel free to talk about local music and hobbies you may have in common. If the conversation stalls, quickly turn the conversation towards the circus. Ask him/her, "Hey, do you like clowns?" Cuz everyone loves clowns, right?

• 15 •

Love is a Sledgehammer

Are we all looking for true love? Can you define true love? Or are you looking for somebody who can just put up with you for an extended period of time, say about 50 years or so? Well, good news for all of us. I have all the answers. I googled "true love," and the first hit was a Discovery Health quiz that will tell you if your current partner is truly the one. It's a thorough 5 questions that tell you correct or incorrect after each one. If you pick an answer they don't agree with, you are told your answer is wrong even if you give a truthful answer, because let's face it – Discovery Health really knows more about how you feel than you do. If you manage to answer all five in a manner pleasing to Discovery Health, then darn it, it's true love. How couldn't it be? But here's the kicker, if you answer all 5 wrong then they think the relationship is doomed. There is no in between. I have more good news. They offer the invite to take the quiz again in case you'd like to change your answers and fool yourself into thinking it may be true love after all.

I'd like to vent for a moment. Communication is key to any relationship. Everyone has heard this. Everyone knows this. Yet, time after time, we choose to make it more difficult than it needs to be. What causes most of the arguments between my wife and I is a question? And here is that question – *What would you like to* _____*?* Fill in the blank with whatever you'd wish. What would you like to eat? Do? Go? Whatever. It ends with silence, frustration, and irritation simply because we love each other, and we want to do what the other person is happy with. On the flip side, we don't want to make a decision at any point in life again. It's a nice bonus having these conversations on cell phones. The delay makes them sound like walkie-talkies. I feel like I should be saying, "Ummmm. I don't know. Where do you want to eat tonight? Over." "Wherever you want to go. Over."

Every time you go to talk, the other person begins to talk as well. You pause, so do they. You wait, thinking they'll get the hint and pick up the conversations again, but they don't. You start to talk and again they talk at the same time. You get like three incoherent words out before you stop mid-syllable. And after each breath, you can hear the other person sighing in agony. Each of you are praying the other will just pick something and then you can move forward pissed off at each other for no particular reason. And holy shit if type of situation happens at the same time you are trying to unlock a car door for someone while they are lifting the handle. Ah, true love.

Back on track. So, finding the right person can be difficult. Luckily for you, I've put together a comprehensive questionnaire that will point you in the right direction to help you find your soul mate. I've developed one for the men and one for the ladies.

<u>Women First:</u>

1. What traits do you find most attractive in a man?
    a. Great sense of humor/funny
    b. Tall, dark, and handsome
    c. Dreamy eyes
    d. Men with lots of disposable cash
    e. A man with a HUGE THROBBING MEMBERship to a respectable a "Jelly of the Month" club

Analysis: If you answered "a" – you're looking for a "good" guy. Have your friends fix you up with the guy that works in their office that typically sits at home watching Comedy Central Friday night stand-up by himself. He's a nice guy, but remember, he's only been laid a couple times so don't expect too much in bed.

Answered "b" – well good looks are hardly overrated. But, you need to be careful. This type of man is often a heartbreaker, a player. Not that you'll mind too much. Your shallow "looks are all that count" superficial ass is just looking for a quick hook-up anyway. Love em and leave em.

Answered "c" – Oh the eyes that reel you in. You gaze across the room looking for that one guy whose eyes speak volumes at a glance. And just then, you spot him. You melt a little inside and your knees are weak. But guess what, he doesn't have dreamy eyes. He's just stoned. Or drunk. Either way, he's going to eat the food from your pantry if you take him home with you and then just pass out before you get any pleasure in return. Sorry, try again.

Answered "d" – Now you're getting somewhere. Men with cash know one thing. And that's how to treat you like a lady. That is, until they get you home and remind you of what money should be able to buy them. That's correct. Pretty woman without the Hollywood ending.

Answered "e" – That's a good girl. You've got your priorities straight. Find a man that is slightly left of center and you're likely going to have a healthy relationship with your jelly loving man. Perfect match.

2. I'll look for a man:
    a. At the mall
    b. In bars and clubs
    c. Through my network of friends
    d. At the Zoo
    e. Online

Analysis: If you answered "a" – Seriously? Are you waiting for Mr. Right to just stroll by with a giant cinnamon sugar pretzel in one hand and an Abercrombie bag in the other and sweep you off your feet? You're more likely to find a lasting relationship from picking up the geek working computer sales at Best Buy. You know he won't be picky.

Answered "b" – Okay. You like the drama. That's cool. Just use protection and remember to get tested. It's everyone's responsibility.

Answered "c" – Probably the safest bet. Your friends want to see you happy and they want to see their other friends happy as well. Win-win. Now you can enjoy all the double dates and activities that your friends are sick of doing with each other, so they drag you and your new beau along to join in the misery.

Answered "d" – Huh? I was just kidding. Do you know something I don't? Do me a favor and let me know how it works out between you two. Send me an invite to the wedding at least. Congrats. Love is awesome.

Answered "e" - Remember that he probably photoshop'd the profile picture too. Don't be disappointed. Oh yeah, by the way, he doesn't really like taking you to see chick flicks regardless of what he wrote on his description. What he does like, however, is the prospect of getting some play. So, enjoy the free movie and dinner. You've got 20 more guys that swiped right waiting for you.

3. True love is
   a. Finding someone that shares in your life's dreams and hopes
   b. Your other half – someone that is the perfect complement to you
   c. Finding someone that will put up with your neurotic, sometimes bitchy self for life
   d. Someone who challenges you mentally and emotionally to make you a better person
   e. Someone who loves you for the quirks that make you special and unique

Analysis: If you answered "a" – Not a bad answer. This person could also be a business partner. Not as romantic, but very practical and possibly lucrative.

Answered "b" – It's nice to have somebody that certainly compliments you and this person just might be your soul mate. But the problem is that they have a drinking problem. I'll bet you didn't know this. Yah, well, now you know. And you cannot just ignore it. The problem doesn't go away just by wishing it to happen.

Answered "c" – Yeah no. This is not true love. It may be your closest shot, but it's not true love. Sorry.

Answered "d" – This could blossom into true love. It could also blossom into murder if they won't quit harping on you to clean up the bathroom after you're done showering. You need all the crap to look your prettiest. And who do you do it for? Him, that's right. And does he appreciate it? Noooooooooo. F#ck him.

Answered "e" – Okay. I think true love is finding beauty in the faults of your mate. Your appreciation for their little faults and vice versa is a sign of real love. Congrats. I think you're moving in the right direction. These special feelings are what transcend us to a new level of happiness. And these feelings last about the first six months. After that, refer to answer "c."

Now for the Men:

1. The first thing you notice on a woman is her
    a. Eyes
    b. Face
    c. Sense of humor
    d. Ass
    e. Boobs

Analysis: Answered "a" – Liar.

Answered "b" – Liar.

Answered "c" – Liar. Come on. No one would believe that.

Answered "d" – Liar. I have no doubt you noticed, but let's be realistic.

Answered "e" – Duh?

2. What stops you from finding that perfect woman?
    a. Nothing. I'm confident she's just around the corner.
    b. I keep falling for psycho chicks

  c. Your job keeps you traveling too much to settle down and find the right person
  d. Restraining orders
  e. Porn

Analysis: If you answered "a" – Maybe that's true. It's that type of positive attitude that could help you through your quest despite the numerous rejections that keeping chipping away at your self-esteem until you're living back with your parents in the basement playing World of Warcraft trying to hook up with the Level 46 Wood Fairy with the screen name SassyPants69.

 Answered "b" – Don't we all. If they've got a little Goth look to them, all the better. Enjoy the ride, but say goodbye to some of your valuables, because they ARE going to get trashed the first time you two have a good fight.

 Answered "c" – Yeah right. Who are you kidding? You're a tool. Change your look, change your attitude, and sell the sports car. It doesn't impress anyone. This is unless you are involved in charity organizations that have you building schools in impoverished countries that need our help. In that case, nice job. You're more man than me. You deserve to find somebody special. Maybe a librarian or that perky next-door neighbor kind of girl. But I'll bet you also play acoustic guitar to get chicks. So never mind. You're still a tool.

 Answered "d" - Don't worry. They expire eventually. Besides, she's just playing hard to get. Stick to your convictions. I'm sure it won't end badly.

 Answered "e" – I'm not surprised. Remember not to click on the pop-up windows on the computer. Those really aren't girls in your neighborhood that want to meet you. The truth is that is you can put your cyber urges away for a few minutes, you may be able to find someone for you that doesn't require downloading.

 3. A first date includes:
  a. Dinner and a movie
  b. A carnival/amusement park type outing
  c. A moonlight walk along the beach
  d. A trip to the backseat of your car

e. Inappropriate first date comments and awkward silence

Analysis: Answered "a" – Okay. Not very original, but tested and true. Make sure you spice it up a bit and maybe add drinks in the mix outside of the dinner. Otherwise, she'll be looking at her watch and you'll be lucky to see a second date.

Answered "b" – Best avoid this scenario. First, you'll go broke playing all the stupid games. And, if you somehow win, she'll be walking along dragging a giant panda behind her, but she'll be thinking, "What the hell am I going to do with this? I'm 24 years old. This shit is going straight in the trash when the date is over." Is that what you want?

Answered "c" – You crazy romantic fool. I suppose you plan on just having a blanket with you as well. Maybe a bottle of wine? Nice try. Are you walking around with a corkscrew in your pants? Let me rephrase that. What I'm saying is that though it sounds romantic, the reality is that all that sand collects somewhere. The movies lie to us. How romantic is it going to be when you lean in to kiss her as you lay on the beach and she gets a grain of sand in her eye? Real slick there, chief. Try again.

Answered "d" – At least you're honest. If you drive a big ole' hoopty car, then you have hope. If you drive a Honda Civic, you best make sure to limber up with some stretches or somebody's pulling a hamstring. Nothing says sexy like, "Oh Oh Oh!! Shit stop! Cramp! Cramp!"

Answered "e" – That's the route most guys take. Many of us aren't the most gifted in small talk and so we get impulsive in our efforts to impress you or persuade you to relax your moral standards. Often, this backfires. Such is life.

If you cannot find the right person for you from these little quizzes, then there just might not be help for you. Listen, I cannot hold your hand through everything. Some aspects of love you have to figure out for yourself. Remember the famous words of Nicholas Cage when asked how he coped with a broken heart – "Love is a sledgehammer, and my nuts are the chopping block."

I'm not sure what that means. I'm actually pretty sure he didn't say that. But solid advice it remains nonetheless. Moving right along..........

• 16 •

Now That You're Stuck with Me

People often ask me, "How do you keep your relationships fresh and exciting?"

Well, that's a good question.

• 17 •

__OK, You're Really Stuck with Me__

The reality is that you're not stuck with your significant other forever. I think our divorce rates prove that quite well. Though, most of us want to hold on to the idealistic thought that we should be able to stay together. Maybe it stems a bit from the fact that we don't want to admit we settled in our relationship or that we continue to fall for the wrong people. Maybe we are afraid to be without somebody. So when you find a partner, you want to hold on to that special someone…..at least for a while.

Here's how it's done. First, accept that you're with this person for now. And that means compromise and patience. Yes, he leaves his dirty laundry lying all over the house. Yes, she's got way too much crap all over the bathroom. Too bad for both of you. Suck it up. As soon as you embrace the reality that the person you are with has faults and you cannot change them entirely, then you can find acceptance. Or, you can dump them like yesterday's trash. Does that help? Do you need a more thorough list of faults that have to be accepted versus idiosyncrasies you cannot possibly live with?

Acceptable Quirks and Eccentricities
- Leaves the toilet seat up
- Licks his ice cream bowl
- Has to sleep with all the doors shut
- Has to leave a "little" bit of light on when sleeping
- Cannot make a decision on where to eat
- She likes to wear my clothes
- Has to smell everything before eating it
- Overabundance of sarcastic retorts
- Answers questions with more questions
- Bites his fingernails
- Says socially inappropriate things at socially inappropriate times
- Bad gas
- Leaves the bathroom door open
- Funky feet
- Have to face the door when sitting in restaurants
- Shares my toothbrush
- Couch potato

"Holy Crap, I will kill you" Shortcomings
- Flirts way too much with your sister
- Calls out someone else's name in bed
- Third eye
- Insists on sleeping with gun under pillow
- Overly paranoid about phantom penguins
- Uses my toothbrush to clean the toilet
- Licks light sockets
- Proclaims that Carrot Top is his/her idol
- Converses with the dead
- Steals money from the poor
- Shits in the sink
- Wears their underwear in the shower
- Refusal to acknowledge that there's no Santa
- <u>Openly enjoys Steven Segal movies</u>

It's pretty simple by my calculations. Find someone that doesn't fall on the second half of that list and hold on tight. They's a keeper, for sure! It's a bit different for some guys. Many a man has been informed that, indeed, they are stuck with their mate forever regardless on his opinion on the matter. Though this may come as a bit of a surprise to him, it is true nevertheless. You don't want to cross a woman that has claimed you as her property. In this situation, simply hand over your wallet, dignity, and your man card. She'll keep them in her purse in case she informs you that you need them for something.

For ladies that don't claim their male property like European explorers landing on fresh soil, you have a different dilemma. Perhaps you've found yourself a man that's no good for you. And for some reason, you want him to be "Mr. Right." But in reality, he's more like *"Mr. Seriously you can't really be into this guy. You know he's just a dog and he doesn't deserve you and he's not going to change, and I can't believe you let him treat you like that. Does he even have a job?"* kind of guy. You women are dumb sometimes. And the guy is going to say whatever he needs to string you along and make sure you keep paying all the rent while he freeloads in your pad. But it's cool, because you say that he really loves you, because he said so. Of course, he won't admit that around anyone else. Whatever, keep holding on. Sure he'll change.

Look, let me sum it up for you. You aren't stuck with anybody. There are situations that lead us to stay with people for the wrong reasons, but often, the lack of contentment that stems from poor relationships pales in comparison to the temporary pain that comes from the breakup. Our insecurity from being alone lends us to staying in the most unsatisfying relationship just so someone can share the hell with you. Hell divided by two is still hell. You can quote me on that. Best cut ties and move forward. Grass is greener, silver lining in everything, etc etc. In you're in a bad relationship, cut ties, pull the plug, lower the boom. And if things are good and there is promise, fight to make it work.

Once you've settled yourself in for the long haul with someone, don't think it's going to just be easy to love someone every day at every moment. We all have our tipping points where we've looked at our precious someone and thought, "I could kill you. No problem." And the best part is that we have these moments and yet, no one actually hurts their spouse…..er……nevermind.

Women – this next part is directed at you. We accept our spouses for who they are, even if they have webbed feet. Well, maybe not if they webbed feet. Ok, some webbed feet people. That's weird. And creepy. Anyway, I've expressed this many times already in this book – ladies, we don't often know what you're talking about. You need to spell it out for the guys. My buddy got in trouble for stirring the macaroni wrong. Yes, stirring the macaroni wrong. Don't ask me how to incorrectly stir macaroni. I don't know, and that particular evening, he sure as hell didn't know either. Yet there he was, wife yelling at him for stirring macaroni. Have I mentioned that he was just stirring macaroni? Of course, now we know that he wasn't stirring macaroni wrong. What happened was that he hadn't taken the time to tell here about something that was going on that weekend or some detail about yadda yadda, blah blah. The problem is that it took one rough evening of guessing games to get to the root cause of the anger. I'm not exactly saying that you need to come right out and tell us just why you might be upset. Personally, I'd rather be in trouble for stirring macaroni, but it must be one or the other. You can't be mad for the trivial stuff to get to the bigger stuff. At some point, we'll just keep stirring the macaroni regardless of your reaction.

Men – here is the flipside. We need to recognize when she's got something on her mind. At least pick up on some of the clues. Then you can start to scrape away at the real problem. It's likely something you've already done, so start thinking. It's in there somewhere. If you can identify it without playing *Bitter Charades* with her, then you may still have a chance at a peaceful evening. Maybe even some good makeup sex. Or, at least a couple hours of channel surfing before you both say you're too tired to fool around because you have to get up early for work tomorrow. If you cannot drudge up an idea of what's bothering her, you'll have to come out and ask. "What's wrong darling," you say. "Nothing," she replies. Don't be dumb here gentlemen. You know something is wrong. If you simply say "okay" and go back to watching television, you'll be making a grave mistake. Repeat the "what's wrong" process numerous times until a discussion or argument ensues. You must get the root cause, which is likely you, because let's be honest. We do all sorts of dumb stuff and don't even realize it. Find out what it was, apologize, make up, move forward and try not to repeat the behavior. You may find out that she just had a bad day, wanted to vent a little, and was looking for you be available to listen to her.

Part Five

Family

• 18 •

How Am I Not Adopted?

Your family is a train wreck. Face it. You may even embrace it. From neurotic mothers to psycho aunts, pervy cousins, and those you'll never admit are actually family, we all have a collection of screwballs bound together by breeding and legal bondage. So how on earth can we all be related? It's easy.

Actually, it's not that easy. I was stuck for some time on this paragraph. After reading the first couple sentences of this chapter over and over, I began to question whether I was adopted. Then I called my mom. She said I was not. So now where do I go from here? Perhaps it's the "my side of the story" syndrome. Every time we are in an argument with somebody, every time we have a beef with something somebody does, our side of the story is always correct. Not theirs, because they are stupid and wrong, and we are right. Isn't that how it goes? So is the way with families. For every moment we've been embarrassed by a family member and wondered how we could be a blood relative to this/that person, it's likely they had the same thought about you. How easy it is to forget that it was you that had too much eggnog at Christmas dinner and thought you could ride the neighbor's plastic reindeer to deliver presents to needy kids in Cleveland because, as you so memorably slurred, "Santa can bite my big white ass."

Ah yes. Perhaps your judgment is a wee bit skewed. However, it doesn't mean you are wrong for wondering how the fact that breeding allows us to co-exist with people that otherwise wouldn't have any reason to associate with us. I think the idea of family is that of comfort and familiarity. It's amazing what you can put up with if it's familiar to you. It's almost inconsequential whether you like your family. We just put up with them. And they put up with us. I have family members that NEVER forget my birthday. They are awesome about sending cards, picking up the phone, emailing, whatever to celebrate another candle on my cake. In return to these gestures, I suck. I've got my immediate family's birthdays down, but from there it goes downhill quickly. I have several nieces and nephews, and I couldn't tell you the month of half of their birthdays. For the couple I do know, I couldn't tell you how old they are. It's sad really. Thank goodness they're family. They accept my shortcomings and are thankful that I have a wife that makes up for my uselessness.

Get ready.....no transition here.

Norman Rockwell can stick it. I'll bet his family was more jacked up than mine. What he didn't put in his art is that the little boy is the doctor's office was there because he'd just stuck a crayon up his nose because his older sister dared him to do it. And it sure didn't show how pissed off mom was after sitting in the waiting room for three hours while the ER desk clerk assured her the wait would only be a couple more minutes. Where's the painting of dad cursing after hitting his thumb for the fifth time with a hammer while trying to complete a DIY project at home? Should I ever become an artist, my first painting will be a dramatic abstract representation of "Timmy as he sneaks back into the house at 3am as mom turns on the kitchen light." You can hang it in your bathroom.

Do you still think you're adopted? Do you think perhaps that aliens dropped you on your parents' doorstep and then reprogrammed their brains to think they had you from the start? No, you don't think that? Sorry to inform some of you that it is indeed the truth. Believe me. I read it in this book I just wrote. Maybe we just wish we were adopted. Then we can use it as an excuse for bizarre behavior or unsightly facial hair. "It's not my fault," you can say. "I have DNA of an unknown source. Perhaps it is tainted from asbestos exposure or acid rain," you will rationalize. And to this, your adoptive family will embrace you in a show of support. They will tell you that they love you like one of their own and that you are as much a part of the family as everyone else. Then you reveal something personal like, "I think I like members of the same sex." Then they will kick you out, but it'll be okay because that will set the stage for a heartwarming reconcilement. That's pretty much how it normally goes, I've heard.

• 19 •

My dad can beat up your step-dad

Oh the way of the fractured family. That's not even a full sentence, but damn it's dramatic. Just sort of sets the tone for the next couple pages of profound thought. Recent polls show that 61% of kids under the age of 17 have a 72% chance of having two or more step siblings in households that share step-parents resulting from the 52% of marriages that result in divorce where one or both of the parents remarry into marriages with multiple children 24% of the time. It's no wonder that dating is difficult these days. Most of us are already related to one another. I guess what I'm saying is that you should go ahead and date your 2nd step cousin twice removed. It's okay.

I was just pondering how our world is evolving so quickly. It seems like we are bombarded each day by more and more sensory input. Technology is growing by leaps and bounds every second. The computer I'm typing on right now is a dinosaur at three years old. Hah, your RAM is only 1 gig. You may as well be working on an Etch-A-Sketch. Society reflects these changes as well. People don't have careers the same way they used to. You don't fall into a job, work 35 years, retire and play golf. Nowadays, you change career paths multiple times. Maybe you're a cop for ten years, and then you go into consulting for a while. After a while, you go back to school and end up in massage therapy school. It's no wonder divorce rates are so high these days. We cannot commit to things anymore. Hell, I cannot commit to a TV channel for an evening. We have 300 TV channels and all I can do is watch shows that are sitting on my DVR. And you know while I watch those shows, I have my phone in my hand surfing social media because I have to stay connected to everyone at all times. Lord help me if Twitter is still around by the time this book ever gets published. Ooooo Oooo, Timmy's taking a dump. Better tweet about it or how will anyone know!?

The whole damn world has ADD at this point. Of course, relationships are going to suffer. Look at the successful marriages at this point. I bet this would be a fascinating experiment. My uneducated guess would be that a significant percentage of people involved in happy, successful marriages use technology that is not on the cutting edge. These are people content with having okay stuff. They may use an iPhone, but it's probably only the 30 gig model. They likely don't watch much reality TV (not that we have much choice these days). You know what they might actually do each evening……talk to one another. They might even still read books. Fancy that. I sound cynical, and I know that. But, I think it's true for the most part. It's funny – I make these broad strokes painting society in a poor light with streaks of sarcasm and biting bitterness for the idealistic world that isn't and yet, I fall directly into the stereotypes which I propagate.

My wife completely digs new technology. Somehow, she manages to live in a completely electronic world. And though she doesn't go out and buy each new toy that hits the market (she would if she could), she manages to take advantage of everything available to her. While she is busy downloading books to her digital Kindle/Sony reader thingy, I contemplate going back to writing this book on yellow legal pads. The only thing that stops me from hand writing this book is that I know at some point, I'd have to type the damn thing out anyway. We balance out, is what I'm saying. I think that's important. I think staying with someone is difficult these days because people have such a struggle to keep up with trends, changes, fads, stuff, things, that it's hard to think about anybody but yourself.

I watch sports because I'm a guy. Nobody stays with the same team for any amount of time any longer. Everybody tests the free agent waters. Teams drop players to save a buck. There's no loyalty on either side. There's no commitment or relationship that lasts, because we're trying to stay ahead, trying to grasp the latest greatest coolest new thing/person/trend. People now more than ever are looking out for themselves before all else. It extends in all walks of life; from sports to jobs, relationships to technology. Everything is built for the now, not the later. It's no wonder relationships struggle to last when everything is stacked against them. We haven't even brought religion into the discussion yet. But don't worry – we'll get to that later. I think I've beaten this topic unnecessarily into the ground. It's tough these days. It doesn't mean we cannot make our marriages work. It just takes a bit of balance and hard work. In a world of change, changing together is harder than ever.

• 20 •

My father hates poetry

Do you have a good relationship with your parents? Do you have a good relationship with your children? Yeah, you love them unconditionally, kind of. But are they also the root of all your problems? Probably. Likely. Yes. Most Definitely.

I was trying to decide in this section whether to write this from the parent or child point of view. Which one needs a voice of direction cast their way. It is too hard to decide where the burden lies. I think it would be easier to make a comparison list. Here it goes.

Reasons My Kids Make My Hair Fall Out
- College Tuition
- Piercings
- Their music
- I'm afraid of the goth friends
- Text messaging
- Little teens don't look like little teens anymore
- Pants falling off every guy's ass
- They won't save for the future
- Being sexually active

Reasons My Parents Suck
- They don't understand that I'm in love with him
- They kiss in public
- Their music
- My parents cannot even check their email without help
- OMG, WTF!?
- They don't know how hard it is for kids these days
- Their car doesn't have an auxiliary jack
- I only have one credit card. What's the big deal?
- They don't trust me alone in the house

Maybe my view is a bit biased at this point in life, but I'm going to side with the parents on this one. I think parents are the ones that need my help more than the children. Not to say that the kids don't need guidance, but they've got time to figure it out. My wife and I have no children, yet this will not discourage me from doling out the advice on proper parenting. You know those baby books that help you prepare to have a child. I believe that many of them are quite sound in their advice. Without having read any of them, I can say with surprising confidence that you are well advised to read any number of them. However, parenting books that deal with your children after the birth and infancy stages get a bit suspect. There are countless books on parenting through the various stages of your child's development. Many of them deal heavily on the direction and discipline of the child. But they fail to often focus on the positive aspects of being a parent, instead taking aim on how much your child can screw up and how you should deal with it.

Send them to "time out."

Talk it out.

Treat them like an adult.

Give them options.

What ever happened to "whoop their ass?" Keep them a bit afraid of you. Remember, you are the parent. Please read this excerpt from renowned child psychologist, Dr. Herman Monroe, entitled *Raising your Children from the Inside Out*.

> *Each child draws from a predisposition to act out in accordance with the level of discipline he/she receives at home. The question of nature versus nurture fails to recognize the inherent ability of the child to stimulate the anger in a parent. Thus, the only course of action in parenting is to yield to the wishes of said child, less they risk the affection of a long-term relationship and gratitude of a quality upbringing.*
>
> *The parent must find an effective way of letting the child vent their frustration and should never chastise the child for the emotional rollercoaster of development. Furthermore, the parent is better off taking a passive role, emitting such penalties when necessary such as, "time out" or "quiet time." These disciplinary actions should also be supported with a tangible present or reward afterword to show the child that caring still exists and parents can indeed buy your love.*

Didn't I tell you how incredibly horrible this stuff is? Who on earth would follow that advice? It makes me sick, really. To think that parents can put stock into beliefs such as that. If that book really existed, I would truly be upset. If Dr. Herman Monroe were real, I would give him a piece of my mind.

Parenting is hard. Damn hard. Even good parents with good intentions produce bad seeds every now and again. I know many parents have a great fear that their child will turn out to be the "guy in the clock tower" or "Cinnamon, now coming to the main stage." But it's not always up to the parents to decide that. Sure, if you don't let your child ever watch television, drink soda, socialize with other children, I think eventually that they'll need to rebel a bit more than most. Put somebody in a school uniform for 10 years and they're gonna pierce some part of their body at some point later. That just happens. As it stands, my parents did a wonderful job raising my sister and me. They stressed the important things, gave guidance when we looked in their direction, and still managed to balance the ability to be concerned and caring without stifling the chance to have the life experiences that help shape an individual. We were allowed to figure things out for ourselves most of the time, even if it was a tough lesson.

I can easily say that my parents were less than amused when I got my first tattoo. They didn't exactly dig the fact that I dyed my hair green or jet black (I'm Irish with a slightly ginger beard) nor would they have appreciated any of the many other colors I fashioned throughout college. They were speechless when I showed them I'd pierced my tongue. "Just don't let your grandmother see it," was all they could muster at that point. But, even when they didn't understand, they showed love. Maybe not support, but love. I cannot imagine that I'd have the same restraint and cool nerve had it been me in their shoes. Not everyone has parents this balanced. I am fortunate to have the Norman Rockwell, white picket fence upbringing.

So where does this leave us. Well, back to the first part of the chapter of course. Dig in already. I'm going to get to the nitty gritty now. We are going to break down parenting into some oversimplified steps. I'm not sure how many as I haven't written the next part of the book yet. But I bet it'll be as least 6. Yes, 6 or more should do the job. Any less than that and I risk my credibility. People will be stopping each other on the street saying that I was a quack for reducing every critical facet of parenting into only 5 aspects. I cannot have that. You cannot have that. I submit that we must go deeper. So without further ado, let us dive in.

Oversimplification #1:

Fathers hate poetry. This is very important. I don't care if your father is a poet. It's still true. Fathers do not want to read poetry their daughters wrote for a couple reasons. The first is that ladies' poetry is filled with drama, love and mush. And no father wants to hear about how their 14-year-old has found true love and the world shall crumble should Cody and she not spend eternity together. Dads don't want to read their son's poetry either (personal experience here). Even the most understanding father would rather their son simply come home talk sports than hear, "Hey dad, you want to read a poem I wrote?" It's just true. Oh well. This is number one for another reason. Poetry leads to parenthood. Follow me on this one. Most guys (the actual percentage is 99.62%) do not like poetry. Yet, we like women. And most women (the actual percentage is 99.62%) do like poetry. And we get women through poetry. Every pickup line is poetry, silk verse aimed to disarm and let us in. Every romantic, sappy, chick-flick date movie is filled with poetic dialogue designed to deflect the clear truth that we wouldn't come up with that on our own. I'm sorry, but Ryan Gosling does not represent the typical male. The typical male needs him to lend voice to our inadequate skills. And it works. By the time you've joined reality again, you are stuck in a relationship with us. And every few months, be it birthday, anniversary, Valentine's day, etc. we renew our wooing of you with poetic sentiment. Everybody should buy stock in Hallmark.

Our relationships are built on a poetic foundation. We wouldn't sniff fatherhood without it. And I believe deep down, we'd like to be good at it. But that is beyond our skill set, and so it festers with us. Thus, we hate poetry and yet, are dependent on it. As Shakespeare famously wrote, "Man is but a pawn. He hath not the constitution for love and flattery. He whose verses stem from false muse may count himself common." He penned this line on a Red Robin restaurant napkin shortly before his death in 1616, and it was recently discovered hidden in a small metal toffee tin purchased by Estelle Wisniewski from a garage sale in La Crosse, WI. Scouts honor, it's true. Researchers also found that after forensic analysis to determine the legitimacy of the note, it was discovered that there was extra text written faintly at the bottom that simply said, "I'm done with this shit. – Willy"

Oversimplification #2:

If it looks like a duck and quacks like a duck....well, must be a bribe? Sponge Bob, mac n' cheese, one more cookie – ALL BRIBES! Parents bribe children ALL the time. Don't even try to argue with me. If you think I'm wrong, put the damn book down right now. Put it down, I dare you. Seriously, put it the hell down. But I'm a good parent you say. Well, I'm not arguing that. Don't feel bad. Just because it took 3 extra months to wean your toddler from their pacifier because at some point you just gave in and shoved it back in the mouth because they wouldn't shut up doesn't make you a bad parent. It's either that or shaken baby, and even I don't have the huevos to insert a joke here when it comes to shaken baby syndrome. I'm just saying that from infancy, kids have an amazing ability to test the limits of human patience. Every now and again, we cave. Whether it's sitting through the same mind-numbing children's video for the 78th time in 14 days (who knew a DVD could wear out so fast?) or offering to pay for the first year's tuition if they promise to not drop out of college. Sometimes bribing your children is easier. It sounds cheap and dirty, I know. I guess it hinges primarily on intention.

There is a fundamental difference between appeasing your child through calculated submission and simply letting them call the shots. If your child dictates what food they eat on a daily basis, buy them some spurs and strap on a harness cuz they're gonna keep riding you like a rented pony. Kids in America are fat because it's the parent's fault. I'm sticking by this one. There are exceptions, sure. But not many. Quit feeding your kids the three foods that they say are alright, and shove a healthy meal down their throats. Do this on a regular basis and then, when you're having one of those days, and your kids are driving you insane without doing even doing anything wrong, you go to McDonalds. No questions asked. No guilt. Just quick bribery. They shut up for a few minutes and you get the peace. It's honestly a fair trade. As they get older, they understand the game. This doesn't mean that your child is in charge. The rules are tricky. You cannot buy them a car to bribe them to stop dating some POS that you don't like. That's the wrong tactic, because they'll just take the car and drive away with that same POS. I had a college buddy whose mom tried to bribe him $50/month to quit smoking. He used the money each month to buy cigarettes. Go figure. But upgrading their cell phone for them with the promise that they'll call from school once a week (and not just because they need money) is a good bride. There's some caring in it that makes everyone happy. If mom slips you $20 to fill your gas tank because she knows you're broke ass, and she also asks you in the same breath to call your grandmother sometime this week….bribe. Call Grammy. It's just that simple. Make mom happy, make Grammy happy, get $20. Put $10 in gas and order a pepperoni pizza.

Oversimplification #3:

It's not Dr. Richmond. It's Doug. If you plan on having a child (especially a boy), take your time finding a doctor. Treat your first meeting like a date. Ask them if they are willing to make a long-term commitment to you as a doctor. By the second visit, just skip the charades and formalities. Gloria and Steven, meet Doug. He'll be the one pulling the crayon out of your child's nose because your oldest dared your youngest to shove it all the way up. Go straight to first names and add him/her to your x-mas card list. We still know who the doctor is in this equation. If this makes you uncomfortable, take the Bugs Bunny route and call her/him, "Doc."

And none of this "title with first name" crap. "Dr. Doug" just sounds creepy. Any physician that refers to himself/herself this way shouldn't be left in a room alone with your children. That's just my thought, and no, it has nothing to do with my childhood, so leave it alone. I don't want to talk about it.

Oversimplification #4:

It's better if you stop biting your fingernails before you have children. Hopefully, this is a habit you've kicked already, or for that matter, never had. But in the slim chance you haven't, now is the time. In your pre-children days, your middle name could have been Danger or Adventure, Entrepreneur or Aspiration, or maybe Marty. But now your middle name is Worry. And that name won't ever change back if you have little Xerox copies of yourself wandering this planet. You will worry about everything they do, everything they are, everything that could impact them. And if you already bite your nails, well, they're gonna bleed for sure. You cannot avoid the worry. I know this is catered to the moms reading this for sure. Men just lose hair. We think it's easier. And if you don't bite your fingernails, don't get cocky. It doesn't make you special. I bet you chew on you lip or have some other nervous worry habit. Just substitute that for nails and keep reading.

There's a second reason you need to avoid the finger gnawing. Parenting is messy and relentless. I mean this in any context with which you wish to recognize it. I wasn't going for the, "Hey. You don't want to chew on your nails after you change a dirty diaper," kind of thought. But now that I took the time to type that sentence, it really makes sense. That's just nasty. I was certainly going for the metaphoric sense as well. Everything about parenting is messy and dirty. Your children leave a wake of debris to sift through daily. You don't get to take a week off and leave that behind. The first few years, the potty training, the mobility of learning to walk (and the newfound freedom that brings) – all messy. But it doesn't change. Trying to get a hormonal teenager to dial down the drama on your everyday parenting decisions is messy. Letting your recent college grad (or dropout) back into the house when you thought they were finally gone for good – messy. As I approach an age that has left much of this behind, I know it's just as messy now for my mom and dad. I'll always be their little boy, and I appreciate it. Hopefully, I give them less with which to concern themselves over these days, and they've figured out when to table the unnecessary worry. And I'd like to think that my mother's fingernails look better and better as I get older. Then again, maybe she just figured out to get manicures.

Oversimplification #5:

Of course they're going to screw it up. Your child is a moron. And I mean this with love.

Oversimplification #6:

Six is afraid of seven, because seven eight nine. That's right. Let your child know that it doesn't make sense sometimes. "Because I said so," is a perfectly acceptable answer to most questions from your child. It even helps to flat out confuse them every now and again. For example, if they ask you where babies come from you answer them in your greatest poker face, "Topeka, Kansas." Offer no further explanation and if they persist, tell them to quit bugging you because the voices in your head will start back up again. Your children will look to you for logical answers, but then we send them out into a crazy world where things don't always make sense. Fair is not always fair. Introduce a little confusion, put up some red tape to simple answers, make them jump through hoops to reach a destination that isn't exactly where they intended to go and they'll be better equipped to deal with it. Just think, one day they'll be sitting in a cubicle working on a root cause analysis report that is due to their Senior Project Manager by 5:00pm but they aren't getting the data from the R&D department in a timely manner because the requisite forms weren't filled out in triplicate and sent to Legal for approval and the Asst. Technical Manager won't return their email and the IT guy says he cannot help access the data without direct approval from the Communication Manager who is too busy pirating music to accept new work at this time. It'll be at this point where your child will be thinking to themselves, *FFFFUUUUUUCCCCKKKKK! This is like dealing with my parents!*

And instead of shooting up the office in a postal rage, they'll just spend their time looking for a new job.

That pretty much sums up parenthood. Maybe there is a bit more to it than that, but I think you're in pretty good shape following these over generalizations. If you feel the need to delve further into the root feelings and fears that are attributed with parenting, I suggest you watch the Lifetime or OWN channel. There you will learn a number of important skills with which every parent should be armed. They include, but are hardly limited to, the following parenting lessons:

- Dealing with the abduction of your child

- Secret parenting skills of Meredith Baxter-Birney
- How to murder your abusive husband
- How to deal with a bulimic child
- How to deal with an anorexic child
- How to turn a bulimic child into an anorexic child
- Accepting your child after they come out of the closet
- Accepting that your child should just come out of the closet
- Becoming a woman scorned

After this, there is nothing left to learn.

• 21 •

Why doesn't Nana just die already?

I cannot explain why some of us die early, why others drudge forward with unhealthy bodies and habits. We cannot decide when we leave this life. You could be conscious of how you live and treat your body like a temple, and still succumb to a heart attack at 42. You could lead a life of safety and still get in a car wreck. Perhaps you believe in God (and I mean Christian God, not sun god, or god of water, or whatever) and you've asked yourself, why do good people die early, and dumbasses live to annoy us all. Perhaps you don't give a hoot about any god and you use this argument to fuel your belief that there isn't any god or afterlife or purpose to our being. The point is that regardless of your beliefs, the wrong people sometimes kick off first and that leaves us feeling lost and insecure and sometimes angry. It can leave us feeling bitter and resentful towards those that don't seem to have any time left on the clock and yet, there they are. It's the old, chain smoking, haven't exercised in twenty years, living off a frozen food diet person that keeps ticking and we cannot explain that.

Don't get me wrong. We don't REALLY want Nana dead. It's just the reflection on those that we've lost all too soon. That pain still hurts. That pain doesn't go away. It may soften with time, but it rushes back in an instant even as I type these words. My heart aches for those I've lost, and I wish they were still here. I wish that sickness and accidents didn't take them away from us. I would like another chance to embrace their existence and make the most of the time I had with them. And yet, those opportunities are gone. All we can do is celebrate each day with those we still have, celebrate our own existence and make something substantial of the time with which we are blessed. It's not Nana's fault, but damn. How's she still breathing?

It's at this point that you can direct all hate mail toward me for battering poor Nana. The truth is that at present, I have one grandmother left and she means much to me. Presumably, I will outlive her and thus will miss her dearly when she is gone. But that won't stop me from wondering why some people last longer than their expected expiration date. This section of the book is on family and not death, so let's come full circle for a moment. We'll move on to death in later chapters and it'll be dark and drawn out enough that I need not continue any longer here less I simply feel like bringing everybody down on an unnecessary somber note.

I guess that just leaves us with Nana again. Do you even know who Nana is? She's that relative that won't go away. Maybe Nana is your Uncle Carl. She could be your cousin Tyler, the successful one that makes an obscene amount of money and arrives late to holiday dinner showing off his new Mercedes. No, I'm not jealous! Tyler's an asshole and everyone in the family knows it. We put up with him because he's family, but nobody likes his trophy wife, and his kid is a spoiled little brat. I'd rather have alcoholic Uncle Carl around. But no matter how much you'd rather not deal with them, they're family. And it's amazingly rare that you don't feel at least a little loss when they aren't around any longer. That's the power of family. Though I cannot explain just how Nana survives in her 90lb frame, still toting around a walker with only one tennis ball left on the bottom for stability, I'm glad she's still hanging on with her old fashioned (very polite way of saying "racist") views. I just wish she didn't smell so much like Ben Gay.

__Author's Note:__ This damn book has taken years to write. In that time, my last grandmother has passed away. And my wife has also lost her last living grandparent as well. So I guess "Nana" has died already. Touché, self-published book. Well played. And yes, we miss them very much.

Part Six

Fear and Insecurity

• 22 •

Nobody Really Likes Spiders

Each chapter of this book should lead you to discover what makes you react the way you do. Each section should help you recognize how to adjust or embrace your current situation to make your life better. And though I openly mock the self-help genre, I am certainly hypocritical in the fact that I solicit your response to exactly that same advice. The only way for me to avoid this hypocrisy is to stop writing the book and pretend the effort never happened. But alas, I cannot. I believe in what I say and the humor with which I write. It serves me well on a personal level and I laugh at my own thoughts, which keeps the voices in my head happier. I also hope to sell a bunch of copies of this book to ~~fools~~ good people that may also benefit from my very limited vision and reason.

It is with that sentiment that we move forth to part six of our journey, the path through fear and insecurity. It certainly seems that much of our fear comes from irrational thoughts. Let's say you're afraid of spiders. Tell me why? Because they're creepy? Well, yah. I think so too. But I don't go yelling when I see one. I don't have to call somebody over to get a tissue and squish it. I just leave the room, pretend it doesn't exist, and never set foot in that room again. Actually, spiders don't bother me much, but it provides the base for my thought that much of our fear is not based in the rational world. Now if we lived in an area where the spiders were often very poisonous, and they sought people out in their sleep and bit them in between their toes – that would be scary. I'd be afraid of that. Maybe you are afraid of clowns. I don't blame you. But aside from the fact that present day clowns are likely weird alcoholic little meth-head carnies, historically clowns were around to bring joy to people. Yet, I think clowns rate high on the "freaks me out for no good reason" scale.

So, what is it about certain things that bring fear out in us?

I'll tell you what it is. The brain produces a chemical known as Trictomanenum. Trictomanenum stimulates the brain to produce the emotional response we associate as fear. The brain produces this chemical naturally and regularly and the body is forced to occasionally expel doses of it regardless of the elements in our surroundings. Therefore, we sometimes feel fear to what would otherwise be a non-fearful element or situation. When confronted by situations that our body is conditioned to show fear or instinct tells us is dangerous to our welfare, more of the Trictomanenum is released. The downside is that the body takes time to reproduce the chemical, and it is entirely possible to run out of it. Our reaction when confronted with continuous or overwhelming fearful situations becomes that of acceptance. The brain is still trying to send the signals, but without the chemical stimulus, the body reacts without emotion. Picture a horror film where the protagonist finally accepts their fate and stops running from the zombies and just goes out, no fear, guns blazing, knowing it's a suicide mission. They are still afraid, but the tank is empty on Trictomanenum. Oh well. Amazing stuff, eh? Pretty soon I'll do some actual research to see is any of this is valid, because it truly sounds good. If Trictomanenum is real, I'll be happy for randomly guessing the name. Until that happens, we'll continue dissecting fear in a more conversational manner.

I think I fear the unknown. I'm not sure though, because I honestly don't know if the unknown is scary. I guess if I know and I'm still scared, then it wasn't so much of the unknown as the known that I was actually scared of, you know? What I do know is that fear often keeps us from making the correct decisions. Fear gives us pause, and in each hesitation, another opportunity slips away. Fear can prevent us from enjoying (or hating) experiences that register emotional output that brings us to highs (and lows) we don't get from every day occurrences. Here's a completely absurd example that barely illustrates my point.

Example – I brushed my teeth this morning.

- Fear level – 1
- Emotional response level – 1

Now, if we alter the variables ever so slightly with a fear element, here's what happens.

Example (modified) – I brushed my teeth this morning with a sanding belt.

- Fear level – 8.5
- Emotional response level – 9

Fear keeps us from doing the insane, but can you imagine how clean your teeth could have been if you had the courage to pull it off. This is assuming of course that you use a very fine grade paper, like 150 grit. Don't use coarse paper. That's just dumb.

Okay, that's a miserable example, so here's a better way to explain it. Day to day routine is typically safe and predictable. Our emotional tag to trivial events, such as commuting to work, fails to excite, fear, or elate. And most of the time, we are relatively happy with this security because we know the general outcome. I don't fear my commute to work. The road is not likely to split open and swallow me up. I may get in an accident, but because I've logged so much time in the car, it doesn't even seem likely and I don't fear it. Change the conditions to snow fall and icy roads, and the fear spikes a bit. The emotional connection and satisfaction of simply making it to work increases as well. If you don't believe me, just think about all the water cooler conversations that morning. They will revolve around how nasty the weather was and how bad the roads were and what wrecks people saw, cars in ditches, etc. You'll wear it like a proud badge that you braved the elements to get to work and sit at your desk for another day of routine. And the emotional high of the "cool" adventure to work goes away if the drive home is the same. Now it just sucks. It's no fun to be put in the same poor scenario with the potential for bad results. In the morning, it was all cool to get an emotional high from the escapade, but at some point, we crave the safety of knowing.

I'm at a swimming hole, and I'm standing on a 20-foot-high cliff staring down at a beautiful pool of deep dreamy bathtub warm water on a beautiful summer's day. All my friends have happily dived in, and I'm standing up there like a chicken with irrational fear slapping me upside the head. Let's breakdown the fear and insecurity in this situation. The water is plenty deep but somehow, I don't buy it. The drop is straight down and there is no loose rock or jagged cliff to slip and bounce off on my way down, but yet I'm certain that I can defy physics, somehow leaping with a trajectory that takes me backward toward the cliff. Highly unlikely. I'm afraid my jump will leave me screaming like a little girl while my friends all looked like Olympic divers exercising a routine warm-up. Possible. I'm most afraid that I will land awkwardly, flat on my back or worse, my face and belly. And it's here that fear and insecurity lead me astray. Like ripping off a band-aid, the problem is that of anticipation. Had I just jumped without hesitation, I would have been fine. But now I let fear creep in. And let me tell you how it all ends up. Instead of embracing that fear and taking it for a ride down the cliff, I try and jump away from it. My fear of the scared, silly face I'll be making in front of my friends for the 1.8 seconds before I splash down causes me to try to dive when I should have jumped in feet first. And while I'm careening down toward the water, I come the realization that I cannot do this, and I try to pull up. But you all know the timeless old saying, "A body inverted is shit out of luck." Well, that's what I am. As I slap the water with my white beluga whale belly, the wind is shot out of me. I paw at the surface emerging to a chorus of laughter from my friends. Fear – 1. Me – 0. Game over.

We face insecurity in much the same way. My wife doesn't like to call people on the telephone much of the time. For example, she purchases an accessory online and it isn't working properly a week after she buys it. She sends an email to the company, but even if they don't respond in a timely manner, she will often refuse to call them and deal with an actual person. It's like a guy who won't ask for directions. We are afraid of dealing with people for the fear that somehow, we will look silly for asking for help or assistance. Insecurities stemming from physical appearance are so overwhelming that I could dedicate the rest of this book to it and we wouldn't even scratch the surface. Plastic surgeons thrive off it. Advertising practically depends upon it. Movies are made about these insecurities starring actors that contribute to the problem often from the stress that society puts upon them. How's that for messed up? I don't even have the energy to dive into this. I believe insecurity in appearance affects almost everybody. It's unavoidable, and that, in itself, is very sad. So instead of devoting whole chapters of the book, I think it best to quote researcher and psychologist, Dr. Edward Block. In this excerpt from his greatest published work, *I am Me and that's all I can Be*, Dr. Block sums up how most people suffer from emotional baggage that stems from the insecurities in our perception of self-appearance. He writes:

> *The overwhelming factor that complicates human progress is insecurity. For people to truly step forward, the abandonment of irrational fear and humiliation must be set to the wayside, lest we choose to never expose ourselves to the judging eye of others. In other words, you must be you. Don't worry about me or him or her, because she isn't you and you aren't him, and he ain't me. If I was you, but not me, he and she wouldn't know you because they'd be focused on me and that leaves you not worrying about me, who in this case is you, not them. Keep that in mind, we'll all be okay. And when I say "we'll," I mean us, which really means you, because that's who you really are and that's all you can be.*

That's deep if I say so myself. Now, who's feeling a bit better about themselves, huh?

• 23 •

<u>Ever hugged a wolverine?</u>

The *Gulo gulo,* otherwise known as the wolverine………..

That's about as far as I got for days regarding the witty start to this chapter. I was trying to get across the idea that is would suck to try and hug a wolverine. I guess that sort of goes without saying and I also suppose it's reasonable to ask why I think that anyone might want to do so in the first place. I have no idea, so let's move forward already with a fantastically awkward transition.

There are some things that no wants to go through, like hugging a wolverine. Okay, I'll let that idea go. How about puberty? There's a life transition like no other. For many, it's about as insecure and full of fear as any time in life. Of course, because of our emotional scope and maturity at the time it takes place, the ordeal of the process is exaggerated to a level that occasionally borders on hysteria.

Certainly, having your first period while in school or being called to the blackboard while dealing with an untimely erection are among the more common horrors of puberty, I like to dwell on the ongoing emotional side of these experiences. Adolescence gives us the chance to feel like adults, all the while not knowing how to deal with the issues. Our relationships throughout childhood usually revolve around proximity. For better or worse, we hang with those around us. Towards junior high and high school, this often changes. Schools get bigger. Cliques form. Relationships blossom. Oh, then comes the drama. Insecurity reaches DEF CON 1 and tears of broken hearted and confidence shaken teenagers rain down daily.

This is easily the worst chapter in the book. I write a paragraph, hate it, delete it, write it again, repeat. But at the same time, it is beginning to illustrate the point of this section of the book. The same fears for which I'm doling out advice are creeping into my brain. I'm afraid that what I'm writing is boring or repetitive. I'm shooting for pithy or witty or profound. At this point, I'd happily accept mildly humorous as well. So I agonize and over-analyze the thoughts that come out. It's different than just going through the editing process. It's more like changing outfits 20 times because "you have nothing to wear" for a special occasion. It's not as if the clothes didn't work for you before, but the situation has changed. You want to stand out or look good for somebody. Writing this book is a similar journey. And I'm sharing in the same anxieties that people face each day, often unnecessarily. I guess that brings the focus back a bit. With a little luck, perhaps this chapter can be salvaged and my confidence restored.

Author's Note: Upon editing the final draft of the book, it is very clear this WASN'T the worst chapter of the book. I read, re-read, re-wrote many chapters of this book that sucked far worse. Lord help me for the remaining dozen or so chapters. Why did I ever do this?

Let's revisit the wolverine hugging scenario again. I know I'm beating a dead horse with this, but my guess is that you're curious how it plays out. I think the odds of somebody being in this scenario are slim. So much so, that I talked to a man who knows a guy who knows some people who are connected. I'm talking Vegas odds (and you are probably aware that all Vegas betting is controlled by the mob). The mob, I mean Vegas oddsmakers put the odds of a person hugging a wolverine on a given day at 46.7 million to 1. On the surface, the odds sound slim, but you must look beneath the surface of misleading information. A large percentage of wolverines reside in Russia, and I've heard that the rest migrate there at least twice a year to feast on the virtually limitless supply of wild turkeys that roam the dense rural forests. Apparently, they taste like chicken. Considering that there are more than 7.4 billion people in the world, that means that there are over 158 wolverines being hugged on any given day. Coincidentally, if you figure that there are approximately 143 million people in Russia, then every millionth person in that country is engaging in some wolverine loving. I dare you to check the population stats. No, I totally dare you. You must assume that there isn't much wolverine traffic in the metropolitan areas, so the odds that somebody is hugging one of these little beasts increases as you move to the rural areas. To surmise, hugging a wolverine is still jack-ass stupid and should be looked at with fear as a totally unnatural act. But, in truth, those crazy f*cking Russians do it all the time. What have we learned from this? Not a God Damn thing.

In the editing process, this chapter could have been re-written. But, to do so would rob you of the mediocrity that is my writing style. Hmmm…..too hard on myself? Not really. This is yet another example of insecurity rearing its ugly head. Self-deprecation is a defense mechanism that, when used properly, helps people head off the criticism faced in daily life. There are, however, people that indulge in this behavior far too often. They're called comedians. Oh, snap. The truth is that all I was trying to get across is that fear is natural. Insecurity is natural as well. That's no reason to sweat it so much. It's hard to think big picture sometimes, but we're selfish creatures. We look out for ourselves most of the time simply for self-preservation. Not only do I "gotta get mine," but I have to make sure I don't lose what I've already got. That's how most of us work. If we weren't insecure, if we didn't carry around as much fear as we do, our lives would be more fulfilling. I think there is a direct correlation to the selfishness and insecurity of people. I have an aunt who is truly a saint of a person. Her selflessness is immeasurable, and I cannot name a kinder person. It's not as if she walks around recovering from a lobotomy with a Stepford wife grin just "aimed to please" at everyone. Quite the opposite actually. She's as normal as you or me, save for the fact that she lives her life to better the lives of others. This doesn't mean she doesn't look out for herself. She just has less to look out for when you strip away the insecurity. I think it takes an immense intelligence to filter through life's stresses and a considerable will to ignore the unnecessary ones. She has that. She has oodles of that. Everyone should have a person like this in their life. Call this person your stabilizer – not to their face, but just in your head. Otherwise, it'll creep them out and they're going to think you're very strange, which you are. And they already know this. So, never mind, go ahead. Not really, but seriously.

If you are searching for these people, here's how to find them. They have the correct emotional response for the given situation. They won't drop the f-bomb describing a movie. They won't exaggerate how bad their day was because of a co-worker. They rarely use "I." They ask you first (about anything). They listen to the response. Here's a biggie – they don't have to tell you about who they are or are not. It's apparent in how they carry themselves. When you hear somebody say, "I don't care about what people think of me," they generally do. Stabilizers (it's a dumb name, I know) don't need to tell you that. It's just how they live.

• 24 •

Dracula Has Fear of Commitment

Dig this, people sometimes fear commitment. People fear Dracula. Relationships can be scary. Dracula can be scary. Therefore, Dracula's relationships can be scary and subsequently, Dracula fears commitment. Still doubt my disjointed logic? Try this one on for size. Relationships suck. Dracula sucks. Ergo, Dracula's relationships suck. Boo-yah!! Seriously, Dracula fears commitment. And why shouldn't he? It takes guts to put yourself out there for someone. It's not as if all of us have amazing looks, great personality, money, etc. Just finding somebody with whom we can connect can be difficult enough, let alone the idea of long-term commitment.

Commitment makes fear ooze from people daily. And we're not talking solely about relationships here. Granted, that's one part of it. But fear of commitment comes from our fear of making poor choices. Not knowing the results of a particular decision scares the hell out of us and that alone makes us hesitant to pull the trigger on simple decisions like what to eat. I think I touched on this somewhere else in the book, but whatever. It's worth repeating. Fear and insecurity lead to poor decisions and a lack of commitment, even in the face of overwhelming data and common sense reasoning. Let's take the commitment test right now.

Question One: You have the chance to visit Europe for one month. You have airfare and lodging covered but only $12 in your bank account. You have a good friend that offers to loan you whatever money you need to cover ANY expenses during the trip. Of course, you'd have to pay him/her back afterwards. Work gives you the time off and says that they will take you back upon return. Do you jump at the chance?

Question Two: You've been dating a person for almost two years, and things are serious. The big question hasn't been popped, but you're both assuming the relationship is moving towards a wonderful marriage. Then, one day, your significant other tells you that they have a secret clown fetish. They'd like you to dress up like a clown during sex. Not every time, but occasionally. Maybe something special like their birthday. Instant deal breaker?

Question Three: You're hiking miles deep in secluded wooded territory, and you've gotten lost. Conventional wisdom says the best course of action is to stay put and somebody will find you. You have a good supply of water, but no substantial food. It could be days before anybody might find you, but trekking deeper into the woods could get you more and more lost. Again, everything you've ever read says to stay put and wait for somebody to find you. Do you stick to the plan and commit to making the logical decision or flee to save yourself?

Question Four: You've entered a bizarre dimension where muppets rule the world with an iron fist and humans have been bumped down a notch in the world pecking order. You're faced with the option of having your innards replaced with muppet stuffing (which strangely wouldn't kill you) which would also subject you to the same problems muppets face daily, such as floppy joint syndrome. Or, do you stay a regular human and face the onslaught of muppet ridicule?

Scoring: Give yourself 2 points for every question you answered truthfully, 3 points for each answer you lied to yourself about, 6 points for every question you ignored based on idiocy of the questionnaire, and subtract 4 points if you answered "C" to any of the questions. Total your score and multiply it by 5. Write that number down on a napkin and then eat the napkin.

Of course these are nonsensical questions. Haven't you read the first twenty plus chapters of this book? I'm just saying that sometimes it's hard to make choices, because choices imply commitment to a feeling, an idea, a consequence. And sometimes, we're a little goofy paranoid about this aspect. Or maybe those questions are simply just filler text to add to what you already know but refuse to admit. I would go so far as to say that the questions are mildly humorous at most. Truth is, that commitment requires an investment that leaves us open to disappointment. There are those that hold back from commitment, sheltering themselves from people and experiences, safeguarding themselves from letdown. Everyone knows these people. Most of them are named Keith. Seriously, they're named Keith. And Keith is missing out on life.

Don't be Keith.

The downside to avoiding commitment is the loss of the highs and lows that make life fun. I was in a relationship years ago in college with a woman named Charisma. Before I get into that, yes, that was her real name. I also dated two women named Candy and even had a Meredith in there. Don't judge me. So Charisma and I dated for some time and it was quite a serious relationship. I can honestly say that the lessons I learned in commitment from that relationship alone made my future relationships much stronger and more successful. My friendships are even better for having gone through that relationship. Oh, you want details. Very well, I will dish.

It's safe to say that Charisma had some baggage going into the relationship. Not that I didn't, but mine was the boring counterpart to that type of personality. I was the normal boy who liked sports and was naïve, raw to the experiences of the world, and sheltered to the alternative lifestyles that existed outside of my suburban upbringing. She was a beatnik poet who hung with people that were WAAAAYYYYYY too cool for me. No idea why we clicked, but whatever. Hanging with her social clique was an exercise in pure insecurity. I feared the way they talked, the way they looked, as if I was judged by my every move. Her friends were simply different from what I was used to. Turns out, I was the one that was judging them, at first it was MY insecurities that were manifested by our interactions. I was worried that my friends wouldn't accept her, or they would pass judgement on me because of who I was dating. In this case, I was right – totally got judged by friends. Turns out, they were insecure themselves. Lessons learned, right? But given this realization and a little boost in maturity over time, I gradually felt more secure of myself and our differences allowed us to grow as a couple. It was quite an epiphany.

And then I broke up with her.

As it turns out, towards the end of the relationship, I was dating someone who had too many issues, at least for me. I concluded that we weren't all that compatible. Oh, and right after we broke up, she knocked on my roommate's window in the middle of the night (thinking it was mine) and hid in the bushes dressed in a black, hooded rain poncho piss drunk after riding her bicycle through a thunderstorm, only to end up crying and barfing on my living room floor in front of my roommates.

Author's Note: During the editing process, my wife put a notation here, asking "You let her in!?" I did. And my roommates were none too happy about it either. But hey, I'm not a total monster. She was crying. I didn't know vomiting was part of the equation.

To say she was batshit crazy is unfair. To say that I wasn't mature enough to deal with the intenseness that was our relationship is far more accurate. Then again, she was a clepto as well..........and that didn't really help. In her defense, however, it was usually when she was drunk. Those are stories for another day.

What I did take from that relationship was that is wasn't all that difficult to get past the faults of people, my own included with some patience and understanding. I found that relationships do not have to be filled with drama. I could bypass drama or simply omit it from my life in many cases. That helped me keep perspective on future girlfriends and potential relationships, also taking some of the pressure off just relating to people in general. As far as commitment goes, it was easy to see in hindsight how putting in the extra effort is worth the hardship or even heartbreak that sometimes comes from it. Whatever. Stay committed. Or don't. Just know that if it doesn't work out, simply moving on is an option. Please don't misunderstand what I'm saying here. I'm not stating that every relationship needs to extend past it's natural and sometimes necessary expiration date. If you have a man that occasionally slaps you around, that's it. End of story. You don't go the extra mile in a relationship that contains abuse. It's not as if you can "better understand" his backhand. Yah yah, domestic abuse joke = not funny. Exactly my point. What I'm saying is that sometimes we don't take the time to put effort into communicating and understanding each other in relationships that have promise. For that matter, some relationships need to end sooner and yet they drag on and on. Ever been in a relationship that you look back on and say, "What the *#@% was I thinking?" Chances are that could have ended sooner. And by the way, others think the same about you. Ooooooooo. That hurts a little deep down. I'm sure there are a couple ladies that gave me an ounce of attention that they'd take back if possible. That's okay. Keeping that self-deprecating fact in my head levels me when my ego decides to speak up.

I lost my train of thought. I think I was trying to somehow make the point that you should figure out why you are in a relationship, or not in a relationship. Maybe you stay in the relationship because the sex is good. Fine, enjoy that. Make sure that it's sooo good that it makes up for the fact that he has no job and you support his sorry ass. If that's the case, more power to you. My guess is that you can do better. But again, if you realize this to be the case and you are happy with that, okay. Just don't be fooling yourself. Maybe you're in a convenience relationship. You like each other, maybe even love each other. The original spark is gone most of the time, but you know each other and you're comfortable with that. Breaking up would be a total pain in the ass and, of course, there would be blame if you initiated the break up. You either just suffer through a boring, safe relationship in which neither is really satisfied, or things begin to deteriorate. Slowly, you begin to disagree about little things until one of you blinks. By that point, you've both probably looked outside the relationship and one if not both are cheating on the other. It is possible that you are stuck with someone because of kids. That's a monster mess unto itself. It's a shame that so many marriages end in divorce and it's certainly tough on kids, but "staying together for the kids' sake" is even more of a joke. I'm sort of highlighting some of the bad stereotype relationships. Please don't overanalyze and try to label the relationship you might be in. Don't feel the need to categorize what role you and your partner fill. But do take the time to understand whether it's right for you. If it isn't, figure out why. Your partner might still be the right person, but they need to know what you're thinking, what you need to be happy, or at least mildly content. Maybe it's you that needs tweaking. Make it happen or step away. My suggestion is that you discuss it with your partner. Have the courage to deal with the consequences, deal with the pain, deal with the effort it takes to keep a relationship going or the effort it takes to end one with a sense of closure.

You may have a great relationship right now. Maybe it's still new and you two are all lovey dovey. Agh, how cute. Let me clean the vomit off the keyboard and continue typing. Seriously, maybe it's healthy and you get what you need from the other. Maybe it's a jacked-up relationship, but it works for both of you. Rare, but possible. Good for you. Keep it that way, but take inventory every so often and adjust as necessary. My marriage is very healthy. Both of our parents have healthy relationships and that type of pedigree never hurts as well. We certainly seem to complement each other and understand each other's needs. That's not to say we don't have issues like any couple. We just manage them. I'll explain with painful detail. Oh yeah – cannot wait for family and friends to read this part of the book. If you are related to me, please feel free to skip ahead. Our sex life is nothing special. It's sparse at best and that is ALL on me. My drive is fairly nonexistent and I'm nothing special anyway. Sucks to admit, but that's the reality. What can I do? I'll tell you what. Listen to my wife and step up to the plate when she needs me to. Put forth the effort and try to remember that my needs and her needs don't always align. Doesn't always matter. I want to keep her happy and I try to look for the clues to make sure that happens. And my wife, bless her heart, is brilliant enough to yell at me when that doesn't happen either. I'm an idiot sometimes and she's a basket case at times so there you go – a match made in heaven. We stay committed to making sure these issues don't outweigh the love we have.

• 25 •

I hate changing in the locker room

Insecurity runs deep in one's self-image. I used to think I was too skinny. I wished growing up that I could pack on muscle and not have a thin frame. Well, I packed on the muscle. Good for me. I also packed on fat and body hair and extra chins when I look down. I stopped growing in height by 14 and have put more than 100 lbs on to the same skinny frame I once owned. I dwell on this. I have tried to diet and am currently on a Nutrisystem program.

> *Author's Note:* I am no longer on a Nutrisystem program. That was years ago. It didn't work. I hated it. I lasted less than six months on the program. It was expensive. I was unhappy. I ended up with a ton of leftover food I didn't want to eat. What else can I say? Hmmmm…. Find another way. What the hell was I thinking?

Of course, I am also sitting in a coffee shop having just polished off a venti caramel Frappuccino. So much for will power. I'm scared to commit to the discipline that it's going to take to get healthy. How messed up is that? Somehow, in my brain I've got this notion that if I eat right, exercise (which I kind of like), and lose weight, I'll be less happy because that means that I'll eat less fast food and soda and such; food, that I may add, makes me feel awful most of the time after I eat it. That's the kind of dislogiclessness with which I suffer. That's right, dislogiclessness. Tuck that made-up word away. It's yours to keep forever.

So why do I feel this way? Same reason many of you do as well. It takes energy, time, and commitment to reach goals. All that effort, ugh! Why can't I just be thin now? Maybe I'm just lazy. I know there's plenty of truth to that, but it has to go deeper. Perhaps not. Perhaps we simply don't really work that hard to survive. If you're an American reading this book, chances are that you are doing just fine in the grand scheme of things. I don't think I have a large contingent of homeless and indigent people buying my book and reading in their spare time. We want instant gratification. On top of that, I think the fear stems from the possibility of failure. What if you try to get in shape, try to lose weight, try to make changes……..and it doesn't work? I mean, really really, doesn't work after considerate effort. Where would that leave your self-esteem? Where do you go from there? That's the thinking many of us have, and it's not fair. It's not fair, because it's a bullshit way of thinking. It's full of self-pity and allows excuses to act in place of reason. We live in a country that allows so many of us to escape from real problems so we can make up reasons to feed our insecurities.

Wow. I just re-read the first couple paragraphs of this chapter. What a pity party for me! That's what I'm talking about. We aren't content with our looks and we find reasons not to do anything about it. We find reasons why it isn't our fault that we aren't in great shape. Then, even if we get in shape, we feel pressured to stay in shape, or worse, get in BETTER shape. You got six pack abs? Well, go get eight pack abs. Hell ya. And after that, don't you dare let it slip. How can you even look in the mirror? Oooooo, I can smell the vanity wafting in the air. I hated changing in the locker room for so many reasons. I think many of us do. But I hate it a bit less these days because I've grown acceptant of the fact that I don't care much about how others view me. I care very much how I view myself and there are internal struggles for sure. I would like to be fit, but most of that revolves around functional fitness and not appearance. I would be lying however, if I said that looking ripped wouldn't likely boost my confidence overall a little bit. There's certainly a level of vanity in me that makes me want to be able to take my shirt off in front of people and feel good about it. And then there is the lack of motivation and confidence to try and make that happen. The argument can be made that keeping the body in good shape is a testament to the pride one takes in self. My body is my temple and all that. Someone who doesn't keep their own body in shape isn't willing to have the dedication to other areas of his/her life. Now I don't entirely believe that. In fact, I think it's a weak argument, but it can be made. But maybe a nugget of truth is hidden in that thought. Take *some* ownership in the way you eat, the way you live, the way you look and do what you can. It doesn't have to be much, but cut out the excuses and try your best. You do that, and I'll bet you can walk a bit taller.

On to the other part of why I hate changing in the locker rooms - Your johnson doesn't belong on the sink top & blow dryers aren't for your ass. The place I worked at had to put up signs to ask the "gentlemen" to wear towels as a courtesy to others. I'd be washing my hands next to some dude that's leaning over the counter trimming his nose hairs while resting his junk on top of the counter. "Pardon me, but you don't mind if I plop my business down on the granite? I like the feel of a cool countertop on my nads while I treat this place like my personal bathroom." No. Why on earth would I mind? Seems quite natural!? That's a talk I never had with my dad. I mean, he taught me how to pee standing up like a big boy. He taught me how to shave and how to drive. But we never had the etiquette chat about whether or not it's acceptable to drop my package down on the countertop after a shower. And yet, I figured it out all by myself. Cookie for me.

And it gets worse. Enter the guys who decide to show their flexibility (amongst other things) by throwing a leg up on the counter to dry their ass with a blow dryer. I wish I was making this up, but I don't have that talent. It's quite impressive to see. Like a train wreck, you cannot really look away. But, at the same time, you can't stare. It's a peripheral nightmare. I'm sure the ladies' locker room is no picnic as well, but I'm not allowed in there and thus do not have any good examples. Ladies, feel free to roll your eyes at my lack of research while you mumble to yourself that you can think of a bunch of examples as to why the locker room experience sucks. I'm just trying to wrap up this chapter on a high note.

If you're the type of person that flaunts it in the locker room, good for you. We're happy that you feel secure enough to unnecessarily strut around in your birthday suit. Actually, we're not, but that's kinda our problem, not yours. That being said, knock it off. It's a fine line between comfort and vanity and we won't give you the benefit of the doubt. Sorry, we just won't. We'll give you a dirty look and talk about you later to our friends and co-workers. Somebody may even write about it in a junky self-help book. For my fellow self-conscious readers, relax a little on the self-image. Chances are that you fit the middle of the road type person and to be honest, nobody checks you out for more than a second anyways. You aren't topic for conversation later. Nobody says, "There was this woman in the locker room and she was like maybe 10 lbs overweight and see looked pretty normal except that I could tell she probably hadn't shaved her legs for a few days." That's the worst water cooler talk around. You either have to be ripped and stand in front of a mirror staring at yourself smiling or be a complete trainwreck with a large hump on your back. Not nice, I know – but it's certainly true. But even if you're Quasimodo, don't let that stop you. Chances are that you are likely mentally tougher than most of us already and you don't need any pep talk from me.

Let's finish this section of the book on fear and insecurity with another list. I've spent the last couple chapters talking about not being afraid or insecure, and it occurred to me that it would be irresponsible of me to not put together a list of reasons to justify these emotions. So, without further ado, here you are.

You should feel fear or insecurity in the following situations:

- You are trapped in a cave with six-year-old who has to pee
- People call you "Sasquatch" or "Charles"
- You think the parking meters are staring at you
- You like Nickelback
- You know somebody in Nickelback
- You use puns……and like them
- Your pizza is delivered by a clown
- You dream job is at Legoland
- Your girlfriend has better facial hair than you
- You fantasize about Mr. Peanut
- You're allergic to metal
- The theme from Cheers plays in your head each morning
- Small children ask you if you're "really" a human
- Your armpits whistle when you flap your arms
- Bread makes you feel spongy
- It makes a grinding sound when you use Q-tips
- Gingers……just gingers
- You have a Velcro wallet
- You have eyes in the back of your head (literally)
- You've named your fingers
- Any of your friends like Nickelback
- You spend a quarter and get a nickel back
- Your grandmother thinks you're sexy
- Your date cancels because she's "busy wrestling with her soul"
- A penguin drives you to work and he smokes a cigar
- Your girlfriend's name is Steve
- Your role model is Stephen Baldwin
- The color green makes you sneeze
- Your breathe smells like leather
- Your social media posts are all armpits
- You cannot grasp the concept of cheese-whiz
- Your shoes walk away from you when they are mad
- You count in fractions

If you are safe from this list, well hallelujah! You have nothing at all to be worried about, ever……..……..except that everyone is talking about you.

Part Seven

Death

• 26 •

Never saw it coming

It's one of the great imponderable questions – If you could know exactly when you were going to die, would you want to know? Most people say no. Some say yes, think it over, and then decide no. Independent studies show that 82% of women say maybe, but they reserve the right to change their minds at any point. My buddy Jason didn't answer the phone, so I don't have any idea what he'd say. Like many questions of this sort, it's meant to provoke conversation about what you'd do with the time you have left. If you had years and years left, would you squander them? Do you squander them now? What if it was only a few days or a few weeks? What then?

Imagine you have 1 year left. Tick tock, tick tock. Where on earth do you start? Do you start going on a bender, satisfying every selfish wish you'd had? Do you reconnect with those that have slipped away over the years? Do you retreat to the comfort of those with which you hold the closest bonds? We usually picture it as some sort of weird freak accident or disease that will soon cut us down. Not like we typically picture it with vivid thought of a demise some 40 years into the future. "Okay, here's the deal. I can tell you when you are going to die. It'll be in 59 years and you'll be 91 years old. You're going to die on the first Tuesday in May. I cannot tell you how, but split pea soup will be involved." *Cue dramatic music......dun duh dunnnnnnnnn*

Yeah. Not how we fantasize death, eh? So maybe it's just better that we don't know when it's going to happen. I put some serious thought into this section of the book. How does one find the balance between death and humor? How is that message conveyed to the reader so that there is a both a profound emotional connection and yet a detachment that keeps you from writing me letters telling me how much my book inspired you to make something of your life? I don't want that burden. Of course this book is an eye opener, and of course you will feel obligated to tell me how much it's meant to you. That part is given. I don't need your praise and admiration. Feel free to save it for person who figures out how to make Member's Only jackets cool again. Yet again, I digress. My research, minutes and minutes of slightly distracted internet searches, has led me to the answer: Death Haiku. Yes yes, that'll be the vessel that carries my message across. We will be linked together as never before, nodding masses that understand the intricacies of a dying grip that tightens with each passing moment. And so I unveil the following:

Death waits for someone

The clock strikes a quarter past

It's time for dinner

Give it a moment to sink in. Nothing, really? I don't blame you. It's not my best haiku. I really do better when the topic is more jovial. Check out this cat haiku.

Kitten nibble pounce

Always batting always playing fun

Watch out hairball hork

See what I mean?

Do you fear dying? I like living, so I'm not a big fan of dying. I think I'm pretty resolved on that topic. And while dying isn't on my list of things to do, I don't mind discussing the topic. It's very possible that I might be going to hell after my ride on the Earthtrain. Despite my belief that I'm genuinely a caring person, I did start a celebrity death pool a while back. Let me explain.

My sister called me one day when I was college. I lived with 5 others in a house that shared one telephone. This was before anybody had cell phones, so the home phone was hooked up to an answering machine (also voicemail was not overly common yet) and that was all we had. If a message was left, it was public for everyone living there. And so it was that on October 13,

1997, the following message was left for me by my dear sister on our home answering machine:

In a distraught voice: "He's dead! Oh, god. He's dead! This is your sister. John Denver's dead! Oh god."

I was at class that Monday, the day after John Denver's passing. I worked after class on campus. By the time, I walked through the front door, my roommates had gathered in the living room, intervention style, eagerly awaiting my return. They looked at me like I was psycho. One of them points at the machine and says, "Bro. You gotta listen to a message from your sister. Something's happened." They don't look as much upset as they do confused, and I cannot read their body language. I play the message of hysterical sister yelling and turn back to everyone. They all stare attentively. I am forced to explain to them that as children, my dad took up playing the guitar. Some of the music he strummed was that of John Denver. From artists like Denver, Gordon Lightfoot, and others suppressed deep in the recesses of my brain, my father would pick away the notes repeatedly to songs that are forever etched in the memories of both me and my sister. When she heard that John Denver decided to see if his plane could swim, she saw the perfect opportunity to embarrass me, leaving a message while acting like a lunatic. It certainly worked, because after I told this boring tale to my roommates, I think they were even more disturbed that she would take the time.

And so it became routine for my sister and I to call one another if we heard of a celebrity passing. Pat Morita kicks the bucket; somebody gets a phone call. The guy who played Juan Epstein from Welcome Back Kotter croaks, phone call. It was a silly excuse to say hello every so often, but we decided that it would be fun to pick a few celebs that we thought might not make it through the year and see who could be a better Nostradamus. I told a couple friends, and a couple co-workers heard about it and before you know it, I've got a whole formal celebrity death pool spreadsheet going. People were picking 15 names, getting points based on age, bonus picks for certain categories, etc. I'm running around recruiting people to play the game and stamping my ticket to hell in the process.

After the first year, I thought about what it had become. I thought about whether there was something very very wrong with participating in such an odd, macabre endeavor. As it turns out, yes. There is something wrong with it. Something very wrong indeed. And, as if participating wasn't bad enough, I was hosting and inviting others to dabble in twisted thought with me. Does this make me a bad person? The simple answer is yes. The complex answer is no. The truthful answer is maybe. I really don't want people thinking I'm this creepy guy who's focus is on people dying. I thought about cancelling the death pool. That would be the social, the professional, the moral thing to do.

But then.........Joe Paterno passed away. And he was my bonus pick for the sports related pick. I was on the leaderboard! High five! "slap"

Don't get me wrong. JoePa's death was sad and I know Happy Valley practically shut down in the days that followed, demanding that Paterno return to coach the Nittany Lions despite his death. So, I decided the pool must continue. Oh well.

• 27 •

Who knew there were so many choices for urns?

Elizabeth Kubler-Ross introduced the world to the five stages of grief, the Kubler-Ross model, which states that people deal with death by processing through five stages: Denial, Anger, Bargaining, Depression, and Acceptance. Her 1969 book, On Death and Dying, was the platform for Kubler-Ross to unveil her theory to the world. The model paved the way for millions to better cope with the prospect of dying or deal with the death of others. For those unfamiliar to the stages, let me take a moment to explain each in broken metaphor and ludicrous example. Please understand that everyone handles death differently (not THEIR death, I mean other people's death – you know what I mean) and the stages of grief are obviously not met in the simplistic order with which I will butcher this topic. Although, if one does deal with death exactly as described by Kubler-Ross, they get three more days to live. Them's the rules. I'll now break down the stages poorly for everyone.

Denial: Pretty simple. I don't want to die. I cannot be the one dying. Go find somebody more terminal than yourself, point at them and say, "See. It's not me. They're the one dying."

Anger: Dammit! Why is my white shirt pink? Probably because you washed it with a red sweater. Oh, and you're dying.

Bargaining: I'll do anything to stop this from happening. I'll eat better, stop smoking, stop watching reality television. Isn't there anything I can do? Sorry, go fish.

Depression: Watching myself die is like having to watch Carrot Top perform. Except dying is funnier.

Acceptance: How surely are the dead beyond death. Death

is what the living carry with them. A state of dread, like some uncanny foretaste of a bitter memory. But the dead do not remember and nothingness is not a curse. Far from it.
– Cormac McCarthy

Now it's tough to think that many people don't waffle back and forth from stage to stage. It's also naïve to assume that people get through all the stages and finally settle in on acceptance. I suspect I'll work on denial for a while, but I'll call it the optimism stage. Sounds a bit rosier in my mind.

Inevitably, you'll deal with death in one way or another. It's also likely that you'll end up having to make the arrangements for a loved one's passing. For many, that's a bigger stress than simply losing the loved one. Where do you start? Unfortunately, making these arrangements can be tricky and expensive. The best bet it to plan ahead. Put down a deposit for a hole in the ground or pick out an urn. Prep a will and start organizing that paperwork. Somebody's going to have to handle everything from your bills to your internet accounts. And damn, does the cost add up quickly. Funeral cost averages go up every year, and now it's skyrocketing over the $10,000 range for a modest service. That's over 10 times the cost compared to about 40 years ago. I don't know about you, but I think it's a bit absurd. It doesn't help when you're dealing with these expenses while also in the middle of the grieving process. It almost seems like a penalty. "Sorry on the passing of your mother. You will now be fined $8,642 for the process of burying her."

Damn, that's cold, but it's the truth. "I see your parents left you a small savings. But the penalty for dying is that we take all that money from you and your dead parents. Sorry. You do get a chunk of granite we shoved in the dirt with their names on it. Have a nice day." *sigh*

Maybe you're thinking cremation. Statistically speaking, cremation is growing in US popularity each year. No joke on that one. People are beginning to opt for the ashes route more and more. I can honestly say that I don't blame them. We're running out of space to bury everybody. Pretty soon we're going to need high rise burial services. Where's grandpa spending eternal peace? Oh, he's on the fifth floor. Take the elevator up and hang a left. Perhaps it's not fair to push my agenda on those reading this book. After all, Shakespeare once wrote, "A man's mind is made not by thoughts of others. He who doth be swayed by the tramps of impression leaves himself an empty fool of mind." Okay, that's crap. I don't know how Shakespeare felt on the topic, but I would guess he'd want you to make up your own mind. So here's a totally unbiased and completely thorough comparison of the upsides of burial vs. cremation

Burial
- Grass smells nice
- Cool ornamental box
- People can visit to remember you
- Engraved headstone to stand the test of time
- You get flowers
- Goth teenagers like to hang out with you

Cremation
- Compact and lightweight. Everyone likes shaving ounces
- Cool ornamental urn
- People remember you whenever they look at the fireplace mantel
- Excuse for loved one to take vacation to spread your ashes somewhere cool
- People assume you're an expensive precious vase (which you are)
- You can fit in overhead compartments for easy travel

Tough call really. I still have to give the tie-breaker to cremation for this reason only. Loved ones can wear a small pendant containing your ashes to hold on to your memory each and every day. In contrast, wearing a necklace with your wife's phalanges hanging from it is considered taboo. Unless you live in New Orleans. Or Haiti. Or maybe Mississippi. I'm not sure.

Plus, when you are cremated, your ashes only amount to about ½ to ¾ of a gallon. If my calculations are correct, this means that if you had 5 Russian nesting dolls made encapsulating your urn, the largest one would be about life size. You could have all five custom-painted from photos of you through the stages of life. How killer would that be? I cannot believe this isn't popular already. I'm all over this idea. It'd be an awesome life sized Weeble.

Maybe it's just wishful thinking, but I'm holding out hope that I can make the time to plan my death correctly. Regardless of which way you lean, save up now because by the time you say goodbye to this world, it'll cost ya.

• 28 •

__Eulogy open mic night__

It doesn't matter whether you've been to one or one hundred. Just about everyone can picture a funeral. It's not exactly the greatest topic to reminisce about, but walk with me through this for a few minutes. Commonly, the process begins with a wake. The funeral (or burial) is often reserved for the closest of friends and family, while the wake is more like the seven degrees of familiarity with the deceased. By that rationale, Kevin Bacon should have 14.73 million people attending his wake. At the wake, anyone that knew you is invited to pay their respects, or at least put in an appearance to make it look as if they cared. Because death is a sensitive topic, I put in a great deal of research to make sure I wasn't talking out of my bottom. I discovered the reason that the ceremony was entitled "wake" was that back in the day, people were occasionally buried before they were actually dead. The thought process was that if you got enough people crying around you, and you were indeed still alive, the noise would be distracting enough to pop you back to consciousness. As medical research progressed, more scientific means developed to ensure that people was truly deceased before burial. German doctor, Ludwig Von Hopperstedefasen developed the "lila nerpschott" technique, which translates loosely in English to "Purple Nurple," a technique that minimized the incidents of premature burial by almost 38%. Many of the European countries embraced this technique until British doctors discovered other means to decipher absolute death. They said, and I quote, "Just toss a how's your papa in his ear and wait til 'e salutes the captain." Nobody had a clue.

Jump back to present day and we're left with wakes and funerals – generally filled with lots of tears and the occasional fist fight. In many services, you have the eulogy. On television, eulogies are reserved mainly for characters not well liked or well known, thus making for awkward laughs on a crappy sitcom. In the real world, it's the common person - the person taken too soon or too late after suffering. It's a dad or a wife, the great aunt you didn't know well, or devastatingly, a child. The point is that it hurts everyone involved. Hearts are torn and lives are interrupted whilst we ponder our loss. A well delivered eulogy can ease the suffering felt and help begin the healing process. It is likely that you may be called to deliver a eulogy one day. The responsibility is large and daunting, compounded by the circumstance that you too are sharing in loss. It's not as if the words for public speaking come to most of us in the best of times, so it stands to reason that delivering a respectful loving eulogy could be amongst the tougher tasks to bestow upon someone. Fortunately, you are reading this book for exactly this type of advice. So, without further delay, I give to you the finer points of delivering the perfect eulogy.

1 – Accept that emotion may overcome you. You may be on the border of inconsolability. This is understandable and you should go with it. Tell people the story of how your father was great because he pulled you from school that one time and took you fishing and he made sure that it seemed like fish were biting, even if he was faking that something was tugging at the line because you were his lil' slugger and he wanted to have a bonding moment and even though he never said he loved you, you knew that in that moment he really did love you, but you wouldn't go in for a hug cuz men don't hug and that's okay…..And all the while, the only thing the mourners can understand about your blubbering eulogy is something about "fish guts love slugger." The reality is that they are sharing not in words but the emotion. You could rattle off a recipe for shake-and-bake chicken and it would have a similar effect with the right emotional dedication. Just make sure you don't pop out a snot bubble. That'll have people giggling when they should be crying and that ain't right.

2 – Don't be afraid to speak your heart. Upon the loss of someone truly beloved, we sometimes harbor anger towards that person for dying and leaving us. Go ahead and vent a little. Just don't vent a lot. "Damn you Uncle Charles for getting caught in a 17-car pileup on the I-65 in a bad ice storm you son of a bitch!"

You *can* point out the faults in someone you've lost. There's a misconception that you have to only speak of the good in someone. It's all right to play both sides of the scale. "My dad's farts stunk so bad that the dog would run away." Wait for laughter and then roll it into a heartwarming memory of how at age 16, he taught you to drive, but ripped a fart just before getting out of the car to allow the DMV instructor to step in and test you. Mesh the good with the bad and let everyone in on a little extra that made the relationship special. Just don't let them in on everything. Nobody needs to know that you miss your wife because sometimes when the mood was right, she be willing to do this little thing with her mouth where she'd……. uhhh yeah. That memory is for you only.

Maybe things weren't that rosy. Perhaps you and your parent/spouse were estranged, and the relationship never got patched up. It might be that if you both lived another 50 years, it never would have gotten better, and you still have pain and resentment. Maybe there's a bit of love of buried deep down, and that's why you are attending the service. Or maybe not. Maybe you're at the funeral out of shear familial obligation. Just because somebody dies, doesn't mean you have to change your feelings. Be as respectful as you can for those that are truly grieving and keep in mind that you can ease their pain in the moment by not airing grievances. Life isn't always pretty. Death sure is hell isn't either.

3 – Call in reinforcements. There are no rules stating that you cannot interact with others during a eulogy. Chances are, any anecdote you're telling was also shared by someone else there. Or at least they've heard you tell the story. Call on them to throw out the occasional "amen" to your story and not only will you feel more comfortable, but everyone else will as well. This bit of advice is simple and yet often ignored.

4 – You're not on stage. It is not a performance and you need to just be you. Don't take on some persona just to add flair or drama. You roll out fake tears or try to drum up laughs and people will be begging you to stop so the dead can rest in peace. Picture Andrew Dice Clay delivering a eulogy. "Jack and Jill went up the hill to fetch a pail of Oooh! Bam! Jill f***in' fell and broke her f***in' neck. Oh! That dumb b****." Actually, that'd be

awesome. I wonder what it would cost to get Dice to show up at my funeral.

Yes, I know that's over the top, but I'm just making a point. Speak from the heart and when you are done, be done. You're not trying to top somebody else's story or fetch the most sympathy sobs. While working on this part of the book, my buddy posted a message on Facebook to me. He told me to include a section of the book that covered "when life throws you lemons, you get together with your friends and slap the shit out of a pumpkin." That message was for me. It means nothing to anyone reading this book. You don't get it, and I don't expect you to. If I had to deliver his eulogy tomorrow, I could use that quote. That's the relationship we have, and that would be why I would miss him. It wouldn't matter that it was an irrelevant inside joke that wouldn't be understood by others. It also wouldn't be worth explaining in the hopes of drawing a certain response from others. Those would be OUR pumpkins, OUR lemons, and we'd be slapping the shit out of them for OUR reasons. I'd probably fess up that I couldn't remember whatsoever what that meant and that didn't matter either.

Author's Note: As I've said many times, this book has taken forever to write and even longer to edit. At this point, I have NO recollection of my buddy messaging me about lemons and pumpkins. To be brutally honest, not sure what buddy I'm even talking about. I have a guess, but it could be a couple people. My friends are strange. Slapping pumpkins doesn't quite narrow it down enough.

Normally, I would give you five steps to eulogy success, but to be honest, I don't have five. I have four. Live with it. I could have given you one and let you move forward thinking that you need to bring down the house with some over the top performance. By the way, if you do treat the eulogy like a 10-minute comedy set, you'd better be good. Have your material down pat and be ready to face a tough crowd. Succeeding on stage in the comedy business is called "killing." And if you're killing at a funeral, well…that's damn funny.

• 29 •

I'm dead, and that's the way I planned it

In times of loss, we reach out to those nearby to give comfort and support, to take our mind off of things, to reminisce. We pick our means of coping, going through the stages at our pace. And even though death is a certainty, it doesn't make the process any easier. When our time comes around, it's the same for those we leave behind. I've talked to many a person that says "My funeral will be different. I want people to celebrate and remember me." I agree. That is a fine gesture, but difficult to pull off. Assuming you have the time to see death coming, you also need the energy to orchestrate your service. And, more importantly, you need those you leave behind to be in on the plan. That's exactly what it is – a game plan. A blue print, a death print, a battle plan. A way to ease pain for those left to mourn your loss. To do it right takes planning.

So, here's my game plan.

It starts with an accomplice. I can only take the plan so far. After that, I'm curling toes and it's left to someone else. My wife, bless her heart, is out. She'll be handling far too much already, and she might be a basket case. I need another relative or close friend who understands that this plan of smiles and fun at a sad time might meet some resistance. Fortunately for me, I have just the person. You might be thinking – Why not go all Andy Kaufman and leave a video for everyone to watch and sing along with and blah blah blah? I'll tell you why – that shit's creepy. Seriously. It's weird enough hearing your own voice recorded or watching yourself on video. I don't want people watching "dead me" telling them to smile. I might have a video telling them there won't be a video. Comedian Nick Swardson had a bit about hiring John Stamos to show up at his funeral to confuse everyone into thinking that somehow he knew a "B" list actor. I have to say that is brilliant. I might steal that idea and not even give him credit, because screw it, I'm already dead. Ooooh wait, I could hire Nick Swardson to come to the funeral and then only people who watch too much Comedy Central would get the reference. Everyone else would figure he's just some obscure co-worker that was looking for a day off.

The next step in the plan involves alcohol. I don't care if people don't drink. My service will be a two-drink minimum. Or better yet, open bar. If we're shelling out thousands to turn my body into a decorative doorstop, we can shell out a few bucks for the booze. It'll be easier for everyone to enjoy the occasion if they're a bit tipsy. In this, I'm a firm believer. Secondly, there will be a dress code. This will really set the tone and might even be the backbone of the whole shindig. NO FORMALWEAR! If you show up in a suit, the jacket immediately comes off, tie is ripped off, and sleeves are rolled up. You come dressed in black and you must wear a Burger King paper hat. Them's the rules. I think people should be as comfortable as they can be during an event such as this. And that's what we're shooting for – an event. We lost a friend some years back and it was the best funeral service I've been a part of. Understand that as I type those words, I understand how odd it sounds, but the service was great. Everyone took turns telling stories, not eulogies. We laughed, cried, hugged, and sighed. And though I know most of my friends (and of course her family) were far closer to her than I, writing now about her death still chokes me up as I type this. I don't want anyone to suppress the natural feelings that come from losing someone. But there was pure joy in that room while everyone celebrated who she was and what impact she'd had on everyone she touched while she was living. So, at my funeral, we're doing that. It's my job between now and then to make sure those stories are worth telling. And the alcohol just makes the stories better.

We'll treat a funeral parlor like a living room. It'll play music my accomplice and I have already picked out – a playlist that'll be a light groove that keeps everyone quietly swaying to a beat without falling asleep. I'll throw in a tearjerker every few songs just because I can *(Cue the song Landslide – Smashing Pumpkins cover. Sorry Stevie Nicks. I hate "death raspy" as a vocal style)*.

We'll rearrange the chairs informally to make it look like a coffee house, and we'll have finger foods. I'll have a short message that my buddy will read to everyone. Yah, I know I said I wouldn't be doing that. Sue me, I lied. But it's not creepy if he reads it. It's heartfelt and genuine and sincere *(Cue any freaking song by Sarah McLaughlin)*. Before people swap stories, everyone will be handed a fat rubber band and you'll all play Tulip (two-lip) Traverse while staring around at one another. The game works by stretching the rubber band over your head until it rests between your nose and your upper lip, a tight rubber band mustache of sorts. Then, without using your hands, you must wiggle all the muscles in your face, tongue, lips to traverse the rubber band over your lips to your chin (you get bonus points for wiggling it below your chin to your neck). Inevitably, it gets caught like a choker between lips in your mouth while you drool all over yourself. I'll be laughing my ass off while watching from the afterworld. *(Spoiler Alert – There is an afterworld. I describe it in amazing detail somewhere later)* Try not to let that distract you from your mission. I've never seen this game fail to produce laughs and a sense of comfort from looking the fool in front of others while they share the same experience.

That's when we start telling stories. We celebrate. We celebrate life. We celebrate memories. We celebrate each other. When my grandfather passed away, we told stories of experiences growing up around each other. We recalled moments from our past, moments that shaped our personalities. Sometimes my grandfather was involved in these memories. Many times, he was not. It wasn't as if we forgot that it was his funeral we were attending. His death allowed those mourning to reconnect with one another in a way that is too often taken for granted on the daily. I don't even have that many good stories of my grandfather. What I can tell you is how his coffee cup looked on the kitchen table. I can tell you exactly how he'd be sitting in his chair while he opened up another box of pistachios on Christmas morning. I can recall the scent of my grandparent's house, room to room. I can remember with striking clarity so many details that came to mind while I was at his funeral. And I can share and discuss these memories with my parents, my sister, my cousins. And they all have their own memories, their own images of what my grandfather's loss means. I don't have too many individual "remember the time when…" stories that involve him. What I do have is a shared connection to those that also congregated around the house during family gatherings while he was alive. Losing him helped us appreciate the details. And so the stories are told.

I got a little off track there. What I was slowly building towards was the thought of just hanging out while everyone had a chance to unwind and remember happy times, regardless of whether I was even involved. If two people say, "He loved to play sports when he was young," and that branches into a discussion of whether the designated hitter is good for baseball (for the record – it is not), I don't care. This serves as a slight distraction and it's a healthy outlet.

These are my wishes. Mine and mine alone. If you would like to have a traditional service, go right ahead. If you'd like no service at all, just ashes scattered into the wind somewhere special, that's cool beans as well. As much as I wish that we all could have years and years of health in front of us, sometimes life doesn't feel like cooperating. And I want to be ready for that. Death plan – here I come.

• 30 •

The afterlife is a rave, so bring your glowsticks

Dare I discuss one of the big questions? What happens when we die? You may think that it depends on your religious beliefs. It does not. Let me paint a picture for you. It starts as the life force drains from your body. I say life force because it's not about soul. I have no soul. You know who had soul? James Brown had soul. Aretha Franklin had soul. Motown had soul. My cracka' ass ain't got no soul. Whitey only has a life force. Sounds as nerdy as if uttered by Obi-Wan Kenobi himself, so I know it's true. So after the life force escapes, it travels through a wrinkle in space where you are met as yourself in human form. Your age is always that of an adult, but it varies depending on the "wheel of age remembrance."

The wheel of age remembrance (WAR) is a spinning wheel kind of like the one on Price is Right. Oh, who I am kidding? It's the exact wheel from the Price is Right, just with ages on the wheel ranging between 20 and 60. You spin the wheel and when it lands, that's your age for eternity. The kicker is that it's not a big deal which number you land on, because I didn't mention the good part. You can reroll the WAR as often as you'd like. It makes living forever a bit more fun when you can just bounce around. Sometimes it takes a while to get the age you want, but it's never-ending fun to watch the wheel go *blip blip blip....... blip......blip.....blip................blip.....................blip*.

This wheel is set up in a town square type setting. The weather is sunny, but the light is more an illumination than it is pure sunlight. Everything is simply bright. The temperature is roughly 73 degrees. For my Canadian friends, that equates to like 3.2 degrees Celsius or something like that. I cannot remember the exact conversion. It's like you take 73, subtract 32, multiple by

5/9ths, spin around until you're dizzy, subtract you best friend's age and divide by pi or some crap like that.

There are billions and billions of people in this afterlife, but it never seems all that crowded. My guess is that there are a number of these WAR's around and everyone is simply zipped through space to the closest one. It's like respawning in a video game except that there isn't some asshole waiting to snipe you the moment you spawn. I suspect that the afterlife is a constantly changing world of thought and we aren't really a physical body at any point. Kind of Matrix-like without the robot agents or the red pill, or the blue pill for that matter. Anyway, after you roll your age and are set for the day, you can bounce around and enjoy the best parts of the afterlife. Each person's afterlife is likely separate from everyone else's, though it doesn't appear that way. You can go grab a bite to eat at a restaurant. The restaurant you want will be there. It will be open, and you will be seated promptly. The people serving and cooking your food really aren't doing so. It just appears that way in your version of the afterlife. Really, they are in their own afterlife, and you're probably the one serving their food.

You can do whatever you'd like without any great repercussion. If you wanted to walk up to a stranger and slap them in the face with a large fish, go for it. You can expect a normal reaction from the person. They'll likely scream at you, "Why would you do that!?" You'll be forced to answer, "Just for the halibut." Then you run away screaming like a madman. It's a long way to go for a poor fish joke, but you just read it and groaned to yourself, so joke's on you. Ha ha. You can't have that moment back. But in all seriousness, there aren't consequences for your actions. If you chop off your arm, you blink and it's back. Jump off the bridge and the moment you hit the water, you're standing on the bridge again. The afterlife allows you infinite mulligans. And because you aren't really engrossed in other people's afterlife, you could push someone off a cliff, and they'd be okay. And of course, you can spend so much time checking in on the "still living." It can be done in real time like a ghost hanging around. It can also be done from a distance, like staring deeply through a snow globe.

The strangest part, though, is what happens in the evenings. Everyone gathers, and I mean everyone, in a warehouse type building. How everyone fits is beyond me, but it seems plausible for some reason. You've got this crazy collection of people and everyone is dressed like suburban judgmental hipsters, but a bit sluttier. Music begins to blare, and everyone is bouncing up and down. The beat starts pounding, *thump thump thump, ooop oooop*. Suddenly, a DJ yells, "Auh Yah! Somebodddddy screeeeeam." Then somebody screams. Damn literal fools. The beat drops and the light fades as bubbly foam begins to ooze from the walls. The light is replaced with a green hum, swirling rhythmically from every angle and it's then that you realize.

The afterlife is a rave, and I need my glowsticks. How weird is that?

And that's the truth. It's exactly how things go down. Scott, you may ask, how would you know the details of the afterlife? Do you have a Doctorate in theology? Have you had a near-death experience where you crossed-over? Do you commune with the dead? No no, nothing like that. It's simple. I stayed at a Holiday Inn Express last night.

Part Eight

Religion

• 31 •

God is hanging out in Cleveland

Webster's defines religion as "the service and worship of God or the supernatural." I define Webster as a little man who says "Mam" and "George" (that's an 80's joke. Fuck you, I'm old). There are so many religions of which one could choose to practice, so many divisions between those religions and so many factors that play into religious choices that it may be mind boggling trying to figure out what's right. For that matter, do any religions have it correct? If so, what does that mean for everyone else? For most, religion is dictated by location. Your religious beliefs, by and large, depend on where you hail from. It's the same for national pride, ethnic pride, favorite sports team, etc. Obviously, this is a blanket statement and simply represents the likelihood that most fall into this structure, but it doesn't omit the fact that we have choices and the option to make our own decisions – even if we lack the ability. So how does one begin to wrap their brain around religious choices? How do we feel secure in our beliefs and the choices we will make based on those beliefs? How do you have faith in your Faith? For that we turn to English poet George Michael, who sums it up quite nicely with his musings on faith. *"Well I guess it would be nice, if I could touch your body, I know not everybody, has got a body like you...... Cause I gotta have Faith."* Never a truer word spoken.

What's the point of religion? Is it to guide us through this life on Earth? Is it to prepare us for a future existence? Perhaps it's too much to discuss in one little book. I like to think not. Let me make some blanket statements about religion. I think it's time to start over. Let's just get that out in the open. We have way too many religions with which to choose. I think it's time to simplify. Let's narrow it down to say 20. You put each religious group into a slow pitch softball league and battle it out over 12 games and a round robin tournament. Winner takes bragging rights for a year or so, and that's where we release our anger. Face it, for centuries we've been fighting religious wars for far less. Wait, let me correct myself, they're called "Holy Wars." And holy shit, are they unnecessary.

Let me now demonstrate my irritation with an irrational fictitious religious debate.

Person A: *I believe that when we die, our bodies go to a different place and it's all great and stuff and we live forever and there's God.*

Person B: *Yeah that's cool, but I believe it's kinda the same, but a bit different and my God is better looking than your God.*

Person A: *Well, actually if you don't believe what I believe, I have a fancy book that tells you you're wrong and that's not really cool for your long-term plans.*

Person B: *Yeah, I got a book too, but mine tells me to watch out for those that don't believe because they've got something coming to them when the time is right.*

Person A: *Funny you should mention that. I think it's clear your line of thinking is skewed, and I am obligated to dislike you to a level that borders on psychotic.*

Person B: *Why are you even standing here? This is my land. I named it and will kill you at this point just for wearing the clothes you have on.*

Person A: *Game on, punk! Bring your best cuz we'll battle this out in a bloody mess despite our constant preaching of compassion towards fellow man.*

I think most religions have it a bit right. They just lack the right PR people. For example, what Christianity needs is a new spokesperson. There's nothing wrong with Kirk Cameron peddling your wares, but it doesn't have the desired impact. Now, if Joe Pesci does a Goodfellas public service announcement telling you, "It'd be wise decision to accept Jesus Christ. Take it from a wise guy like me……or I'll beat your ****** head in you little ********* ********." That's a message that's hard to ignore.

Maybe you think Buddhist teachings are your spiritual calling, but you're not sure because chances are you're an American reading this and well…..you're uneducated and clueless about what Buddhism even is. It's okay, nobody expects much from you. That's why you only speak English. Those two semesters of Spanish didn't teach you much anyway unless you want to know where the bathroom is. Oh, you took French or German. Way to piss away your education. Cool that you can count to ten. Now focus back in because I'm laying down the real scoop. Where was I? Oh, Buddhism, that's right. So you think it's all cool because Buddha's all peaceful sitting there in the Lotus position? Chubby looking Buddha dude looking all peaceful humming "ooooohhhhhhmmmmmmmmmmm" to himself and you picture yourself at peace with the world. Maybe you even have a yin-yang tattooed on your left ankle.

Author's Note: I have a yin-yang tattooed on my left ankle. It's set inside of tribal. Yep. We all make poor life choices. Mine was to get a tattoo at 2am on Thanksgiving in Chicago.

What you don't know is that Buddha was a skinny ass guy, yin and yang are Chinese and really don't mean a thing as it pertains to traditional Buddhist beliefs, and the core of Buddhist teachings revolve around the existence of suffering and how it affects us.

I know it's not really what you thought it was. That's exactly what I'm saying. We need to modern it up a little. Let's go with Biggest Loser, Buddhist edition. We'll go from "Laughing Buddha" (the fat monk you mistook for Buddha) to Siddhartha Gautama (the spiritual teacher who founded Buddhist faith. We bring in Jillian Michaels to scream the Four Noble Truths at them while our fat American butts get a little spiritual education. Picture it – episode begins with Laughing Buddha not so smiley on a treadmill sucking wind at a whopping 2 miles per hour while Michaels is barking, "Life IS suffering. Suffering arises from attachment!" Then we get a huge montage that climaxes with Buddha finally pulling the second leg over the first in Lotus and everyone cries and claps as the scale reveals that Buddha has dropped an astonishing 162lbs from fasting alone. The doctors lecture him that a healthy diet is the key to keeping the weight off and everyone walks away hand in hand contented in the belief that Buddha has found the Middle Path. That's TV gold. Put it up against any reality show, I don't care. It'll hold strong.

I shall ramble on. With soooooo much debate on religion, how can you make a simple choice? You cannot. There isn't anything simple about a belief structure. Religion has been the cause of war, death, and hate between millions of people. You're an atheist, you say? That's still a belief structure. And people don't like you any more for it. Okay, maybe I do.

Can you imagine what would happen if we knew what the truth was? Can you even comprehend what would happen if some God came down and was like, "Yeah, so this stuff is getting a bit out of hand. Sorry, I've been busy, but I guess this a bit overdue. Here's the scoop. You die and then you join me here in the afterlife. It's pretty crowded out here, so we have a lot of high-rise apartments. Basically, we all kinda sit around and do nothing but watch those still living like reality TV. It's boring, but on Tuesdays, I make meatloaf for everyone and that keeps eternity from getting too stale. Any questions?"

Not only would that blow everyone's mind, but we'd have to find another reason to dislike one another. Don't worry, we would. People kinda suck that way. And at that point, this God would also be screwed because once you show yourself, it's hard to disappear again. To be honest, it'd be beyond difficult just to get people to believe that you're the only God. You'd have to make more than a convincing argument. We're talking better than magician card tricks. It'd have to be a global announcement, like, clouds taking shape in your form all around the world kinda big. It's not like you could even go internet, because people would immediately be calling "fake news" on that. And people would start getting critical of God and why he didn't show up earlier and why he lets bad things happen. God would seriously have to be like, "Look, I created this shit. After that, it was on you."

OR.......

Maybe there are ALL the Gods that we currently believe in. And, they all get along well. They hang out all the time and their biggest issue is how people cannot simply treat each other with kindness and respect and love. But the Gods have grown tired of our antics and they only have one representative hanging with us at any given time. One God to sort of look things over, step in occasionally, smite a fool or two. You know, the basics. The rest of the Gods are chillin' elsewhere, checking in on life forms from other planets that are more advanced than us. Earth is like a 6-year-old that hasn't had any discipline and now thinks that everything can be gained with a big-enough temper tantrum. And the God that draws the short straw must hang out somewhere while he's babysitting. And that somewhere is Cleveland. Don't question this. There are bigger mysteries in the world. And God has a Podcast. And anybody can listen to it through any device they wanted. Literally, anything. If you want Godcast Podcast, you can pick up a tin can, tilt it to your ear, and BOOM, podcast. Some people say that a shoe is the best way to listen. Apparently, the acoustics are fantastic. Some call it Diety-wifi. Others simply call it magic. God calls it Steve. He has a weird sense of humor.

• 32 •

Jesus needs a cape

I think the appearance of Gods matters. Take the Greek and Roman Gods for example. They flexed their muscles, put on armor and really dressed the part to look tough. In contrast, you have Christianity. I know, you likely think I'll keep going down this path. You're probably correct in these assumptions. Perhaps I'll take the time while editing to fill this section in a bit, but for now, I'll keep referencing Christianity in comparison to other religions. I do this because primarily because I was raised a Christian, Catholic no less, and because I don't know that much about other religions. I probably don't have an intelligible grasp on Catholicism either. But that's par for the course. Back to the appearance issue. It's believed that we cannot see God in all his glory because we are sinners. God is simply a spirit. This could be true. Perhaps we cannot comprehend God's appearance because we lack the capacity to a higher level of majesty. That's why we need some sort of anthropomorphic appearance of God. But, here is what I believe. If God (emphasis on IF) exists, he can just as easily choose to let us see him in all his glory. He can open our eyes to his greatness. The fact that he appears to us as a bush or a stain on a wall is just to hide the truth. The truth is that God looks pretty much like Robert Loggia. Yep, Robert Loggia. Who would have guessed? As it turns out, he picked that face when he created everything back in the day and didn't really think about how we would judge looks after the first 3.5 million years on earth. Of course, he has the power to look like whatever he'd like, but when God is kicking back in his lazy boy recliner cloud watching old episodes of Highway to Heaven next to Michael Landon, he does so looking like good ole' Loggia. And this is great contrast to everything we think of when it comes to Zeus or Ares or Poseidon. Those guys were jacked. You know Zeus was on roids. No god should be that shredded. It seems like most gods are either indescribable or are cartoon muscled. There should be some common ground. I think this is why Jesus was a pretty popular guy, shredded but skinny - like Brad Pitt in Snatch.

The son of God was a little bit easier for us to wrap our brain around. It's like God was like, "Okay, I need something that people can grasp. Hmmmm. The humans can't dig my awesomeness without their heads exploding. How about I carve out a son from scratch? Sure, why not." But then he thought people would still have their minds blown if he just created a son "*poof*", so he went a different route. Many believe Mary was chosen because of her blood line and some believe that Mary herself was born from Immaculate Conception after a prayer from her barren mother was answered. Some believe that Mary was just a good person and deserving of carrying the son of God. The reality was that Mary had signed up for the annual goat giveaway contest in Bethlehem. Tammy Peuterschmidt ended up winning, but second prize was impregnation by God, of which Mary won. Third place was for a free 20oz frozen smoothie from the Banana Pit which was never used because Abraham Jones claims that he didn't received it in the mail. A response from representatives at the Banana Pit was never recorded on paper and thus it remains a great mystery today. What does this all boil down to? Well, Jesus of course.

Jesus needs a cape. The robes just don't do him justice. I mean, don't get me wrong. He turns water into wine, and that's a hell of a cool party trick. Can you imagine hanging with him swapping stories about your day? You'd be like, "Oh man. My day was rough. We spent hours trying to get the last few stones in place building the east wall of the church." And Jesus would be standing there all humble and shit like, "Yeah. I just cured a leper today - pretty boring day actually." All the while you're just thinking, Jesus Christ, put a cape on or something so it's obvious. You're making us all look bad!

My guess is that Jesus wanted a cape, but his apostles talked him out of it. One day, Jesus comes in with a cape flowing behind him all nonchalant and his boys are like, "Uh, Big J. Can we have a word? What's with the cape?" Jesus would play it off all cool, saying it wasn't a cape. It was a simply a cloak and it was because it was cold out this morning. Bartholomew would say,

"Jesus, it really looks like a cape. It's blue with gold trim and it has a giant J on it written like a lightning bolt?" Jesus would be like, "Nope. It's a cloak." And Judas would mumble under his breath, "You dick. It's made of shiny Rayon." "I'm sorry. Did you have something to add, Judas?" Jesus would bark. In the end, Jesus would decide against the cape, but that doesn't mean it was the correct decision. Imagine if Jesus went forward with the fashion choice, it probably would have escalated. It wouldn't be long before he ditched the sandals for a proper pair of boots. And you know he'd have to get a mask. We'd basically have our first super hero. Or maybe not. I don't know. Perhaps I'm wrong. Jesus doesn't need a cape.

• 33 •

I have a fork, just need an outlet

Speaking about religion can be difficult for many. It's often as appealing as talking politics. If you disagree, hang out at a social function and kick off some conversation with, "So, what god do you follow?" Substitute the word "god" in that statement for the words "sports team" and you'd get a whole different response. At worst, somebody might tell you that they don't really like sports. They'll be less comfortable saying they don't really like god. Writing about religion isn't much easier. But we're going to grind along anyways.

My intention was to discuss religion from the view of mental health and benefit. What does religious belief, or lack of, give people? I absolutely envy those who hold a strong belief regardless of what that belief may be. I haven't ever been able to make up my mind on the matter. Perhaps I'll have an epiphany one day and know what direction to follow. It'll be on a Tuesday and I'll be walking down 17th Ave when a piano being lifted via some ridiculously uncommon pulley system suddenly breaks and comes crashing down. I'd like to be the guy that then saves the beautiful girl from getting crushed, but the reality will be that it's me getting pushed to safety by a sweaty moving van employee who was supposed to be helping the hoist up the piano. Yep. That's exactly how I envision it. I will walk away from this close brush with death and realize the truth about fate and destiny. I will come to grips with all the questions I had about faith. Everything will be clear for the briefest of moments. But damn my ADD, I'll forget it all two seconds later when I sit back and think, "Where the hell were they going with that piano? Seriously, like it was going to fit in a window. Who really has a grand piano living in a fifth-floor studio apartment? Is this some ACME looney toons crap?" I'll ponder that for the next couple hours while I stop off and grab a hot dog for lunch, and just before I settle in at my desk for the second half of a work day that is dragging on, I'll think, "Oh, wait. I had life all figured out there for a second. Damn. Maybe it'll come back to me."

If I put religious belief on a scale, with 1 being unabashed atheist and 10 being "crazy eyed" devoted to their religion, I tend to favor people between 2 and 7. Those that would consider themselves a 1 on the scale maybe need to just relax and invite the absurd into their life a bit more. They also need to reconsider my whole Robert Loggia hypothesis from a couple chapters ago. That's worth having a little faith. A 2 is still pretty sure that jack squat happens after we die. 7 on the scale is reserved for those that have solid faith, believe their religion to be true in its teachings, and would invite others to share in that belief (if others expressed interest). If you start actively recruiting, you're pushing into the 8 category. Step it back there buddy. Didn't you see the "no soliciting" sign on my door? Please take my phone number off your list. No thanks, I don't want a little bible. By the time you hit a 9 or 10 on the list, I don't even want you reading this book for fear you'll protest the existence of this book or put a bullet in my brain. Just in case you aren't sure how to categorize yourself, I have once again put together a scientific questionnaire that accurately defines your standing on the scale. Pick the most appropriate answer to the following questions/situations that encapsulates your feelings.

Question #1 - A man's hat blows off in the wind in a crowded urban setting. While chasing his hat, he trips on the curb and eats pavement. He's scratched up his knee and palms, but nothing too major. His hat is run over by a taxi and it's pretty well ruined. He yells "God Dammit" and limps away out of view.

- a. God had nothing to do with it. That was funny shit.
- b. I don't think God really played a role in this. I probably should have helped him get his hat or at least seen if he was okay
- c. Oh, damn. I can't believe with all these people around that nobody grabbed his hat. I would have, but I was busy laughing my ass off. Mean, I know.
- d. God did that as a test to see if you would use his name in vain. You failed. Prepare for hell.

Question #2 – You find $50 laying on the floor of a laundromat. What do you do?

    a. Finders keepers.
    b. I look around for somebody who might have lost it. I don't say anything, but honestly, I look pretty hard. I mean, come on, how can you really tell who might have dropped it. I'll keep it, but I'll feel bad for the person that dropped it.
    c. I pick it up slowly take it back to my seat and drop it casually next to my feet. Then somebody eventually points it out to me, saying "Hey man. Did you drop that?" Then it looks like it was my $50 the whole time.
    d. Finders keepers. God said so.

Question #3 – Assuming for the context of this question that there is an afterlife, "Who would you want to have as your tour guide?"

    a. Alex Trebek. Hell isn't complete without him, and he'll tell you every f****** fact about it.
    b. Adam Savage from Mythbusters. He's an atheist. If it turns out that there's an afterlife, we'll need to start running some tests to see if we can confirm that we're really in it. Can an afterlife be blown up with enough C-4?
    c. Gene Wilder as Willy Wonka. And the rowers will keep on rowing.
    d. Billy, the creepy puppet riding the bicycle from the Saw movies. And you'll hold his hand every step of the way.

Question #4 – You meet a deity while walking down a deserted alley late at night. You knowingly accept that he/she/it is a deity. Again, this is my book. You must accept it or stop reading. Fine, you know it's a deity because you feel it deep down and their physical appearance is that of royalty mixed with glowing divinity. Does that help? Anyway, the deity asks you to perform something as close to a miracle as you've got in you. Do you:

a. Wet yourself in the presence of a deity, babble a bit and pass out.
b. Download a free Pocket Money app for your iPhone and try to balance the US budget.
c. Find the nearest Kardashian and take 'em out for humanity's sake.
d. Vow to be a better person from this day forward
e. Attempt to cure a major disease like malaria, but settle for stifling something like conjunctivitis (cuz really, nobody is going to pick answer D)

Question #5 – Your religious views would be swayed if:

a. The zombie apocalypse happens
b. Nuclear war happens
c. The Pope was caught in a sex scandal with a Victoria Secret model
d. It turns out that every religious text when read aloud syncs up with Floyd's Dark Side of the Moon

Question #6 – If there is no afterlife, what do you think is most likely to happen in your mind just a split second before you die?

a. Nothing. Simply fade to black
b. A flash of white light, a glimmer of hope that there is something beyond before you blink out
c. As in the cliché, your life's story flashes before you in an instant forming a nice little recap before the end
d. God appears, gives you a quick smile, and yells "Fooled ya!"
e. An image of a midget cowboy riding an ice cream rocket flashes before your eyes. All you can think is *What the …..?* and poof, life is over

Here's how the scoring works. Take out a pencil or pen to keep score if you'd like, because the calculation system works better if you do it in the correct order. Based on my religious scale from earlier in the chapter, give yourself a starting number. For question 1, give yourself 2 points if you answered A, 1 point if you answered B, 4 points if you answered C, and 7 points if you answered D. For question 2, 2 points for A, 3 points for B, subtract 2 points for C, subtract 5 points for D. For question 3, 1 point for A, 9 points for B, 10 points for C, zero points for D. For question 4, subtract 5 points for A, subtract 7 for B, add 4 points for C, 6 points for D, and 10 points for E. For question 5, zero points for A, zero points for B, subtract 7 for C, subtract 1 for D. Still with me? No kidding? Ok, take your answer and divide it by 0, then add back the original number with which you started, because these questions won't really tell you a damn thing about your religious beliefs. By now, hopefully you've figured out the trend in this self-help book. I'm here to entertain and lay down some friendly advice to help live a pleasant journey. If you are still humored by this nonsense, then please read on for there isn't much to go and we'll get to the bottom of religious thought once and for all.

• 34 •

I walk the path, but I think I stepped in something

I debated whether to add the religious section to this book for some while. In the end, I felt it necessary to include religion for one reason. It would be wrong not to. I like religion. I like discussing religion with people. Not debating religion, but rather discussing it. I admit that I know very little. Being raised Catholic, it's easy to poke fun in that direction. Picking on Catholics isn't exactly uncharted territory, and it's not going away any time soon. Perhaps if we relax the whole stance on the celibacy in the priesthood and sisterhood, we'll make progress again. If God exists as in the Catholic eyes, I'll be looking for answers to that question first. I once asked an elderly sister of the parish who had shown devotion to God and the church for over 60 years, "How much closer do you feel to God after all these years of service." She answered, "Nun."

Ha ha ha ha

Okay, that joke just came to me, and nobody can resist a bad pun, a nun-pun. Where was I? Ah yes, Catholic faith and it's fine direction. That was my upbringing. I went each Sunday to church. I learned when to kneel, when to stand, how to make it look like I was singing without singing. I shook hands with strangers each week offering awkward "peace be with you" to four or five people until I could sit back down and focus on the countdown to the end of mass. I went to CCD, went through Communion and Confirmation, ate the stale wafer and basically went through the motions. My parents didn't push religion on me very hard. The need for religious fulfillment never really reached me. I couldn't help but look at it from a simplistic approach. There might be or there might not be. I don't know. I also grew up around a bunch of Christian people. I didn't know what other faiths existed or who believed in what. What I do know is that people do believe. They find God in tough times. They find God in family. They find direction for daily living. I think this is wonderful. Religious following gives you a pathway to lead your life, but it doesn't come without a few questions.

I strongly strongly strongly believe that faith should be questioned. Did I mention the strongly part? Atheists, listen up to this part as well. Even though you may be set in your ways, that just puts you on the visitor's side of the stadium bleachers. You're still at the game. Questioning your faith (or lack of) is a good thing. Questioning allows to see if the path on which you tread is one worth walking. If your faith is strong, this will reaffirm your dedication and keep you feeling confident in the choices you've made. If you find your faith lacking when you begin to question, then it is time for more questions. Perhaps you've chosen the wrong path. And by that, I don't mean the wrong religion. I am also not implying that it means that you'll be agnostic, atheist, or anything else for that matter. It simply means you'll continue to be a free thinker. Open minds see more. Open hearts feel more. If you cannot discuss your faith for fear that you'll be "swayed" in another direction, I argue that you are already swayed. Be open to the views of others and you'll find validation in your own choices or the freedom to change your mind. What makes your religion right? Does that mean that others are wrong? How can you be sure there isn't a god? And agnostic people out there, you don't get off easy as well. I know far too many people that are like, "I'm agnostic, because I just don't know. There might be a god, but I just cannot make up my mind." BULLSHIT!!! You're too lazy and too scared to pick a faith and think it could be right. Study Taoism and tell me you don't feel a bit better about a yin-yang. Pick up a copy of the Koran and learn a little something. Then make some decisions. Maybe it'll all click, and you'll have a blueprint that guides you through a sense of enlightenment and lifts you to levels you would otherwise never achieve.

Voltaire is famously quoted as saying, "I disagree strongly with what you say, but I'll defend to the death your right to say it." This philosophy should be embraced for more often than it is. Humans will never agree on one view, one absolute, one right or one wrong. We won't. We simply.....just.....will..... not, ever.

And so, we will carry forward with varying thoughts and varying beliefs. We will speak of these thoughts for we have mouths, and language and communication are necessary. Oh, but then when we hear opposing thoughts, we have tension. "My religious upbringing teachers me that……" "Well your religion is a fairy tale of lies and unrealistic………" As the crowd builds, Voltaire is jumping up in the back yelling, "Uh, hey guys. About that whole defend to the death stuff, yah, we're headed in that direction. Maybe I should have refined that thought." The trouble is that cool famous quotes must be somewhat short, and what you don't know was that Voltaire made a small amendment to the quote just before his death in 1778. The statement then read, "I disagree strongly with what you say, but I'll defend to the death your right to say it. Let's just not get carried away, eh?" I'm just saying that you can make a statement like you think pistachio is the best flavor ice cream, but that doesn't mean I have to agree with it. Cuz, seriously, pistachio? I don't think so. Let us not forget however, that free speech is not without consequence. While you have the right to say whatever you'd like, understand that others might not want to hear it. And if you exercise free speech to its limits, you'll find that out quickly. You can tell your boss to F-off any time you'd like. That's your prerogative. Your boss can inform you that you no longer work for this establishment. That's his/her prerogative. We could do a whole section on free speech, but I'm way off topic right now. I'm gonna bring us back to religion.

As it pertains to matters of faith, go forth in whichever direction you wish. If you think you're right and everyone is wrong, fine by me. Remember though, if your thoughts and my thoughts don't jive, it isn't a reason for the world to come to a grinding halt. "Can't we all just get along?" Well, no. We cannot. But we can try. And by trying, we can avoid unnecessary arguments. We can avoid unnecessary hate. To increase tolerance and understand is to decrease bloodshed and war. I believe religion to be far bigger than how we generalize it – which god is your god? You don't believe in one? Etc etc etc…..

I think if we didn't fear death or we knew what was next, we might have a different take on religion. But that's not going to change. We need a reason to be good in this life. Some hold to the thought that this is only life we get, so we may as well make the most of it. Some hold to the same thought, so what's the point of being good if you just die and blink out? That's the simple "glass half full" people versus the "glass is never going to be full so what's the f****** point?" people. Maybe your belief is that if you're good, you'll be reincarnated in better form. Maybe you figure that if you're an a-hole in this life and you come back as a cockroach, you won't remember it anyway, so again, what's the point in putting out the effort? My religion thoughts are still undecided. If you'd like to persuade me to walk a few steps in your direction, I'd happily do so. I get what I put into this life. I get peace and happiness in doing what I can to enjoy my existence. I feel content in knowing that I care about others. I give a little but know darn well that I could give more without much sacrifice. I pick my battles to fight for causes in which I believe. I don't stress in trying to save the world or have it all figured out without religious guidance. I think not knowing bothers people. To quote the philosopher Lloyd Dobler, "How many of them really know what they want, though? I mean, a lot of them think they have to know, right? But inside they don't really know, so... I don't know, but I know that I don't know."

Well said Lloyd. Remind me to borrow a copy of your Hey Soul Classics someday.

Part Nine

Bringing Closure

• 35 •

Gimme some tongs, I'm making a life salad

Do you have any regrets? Only 2, that's pretty good. I won't bother to ask you if you had a chance to do it again, would you do it differently. It really doesn't matter. Some people might say no way, for fear that it might lead them in a different direction and then they wouldn't have been at a certain place to meet a certain person or whatever. Or maybe you'd say that you'd change a few important, embarrassing or regretful decisions. But this is supposing that you'd somehow know better than you did the first time. If we simple rewound time, you'll pull the same crap you did the first time, so that doesn't help any. In fact, by that rational, perhaps you have had a second chance before. In that case, way to screw up twice. Nicely done. I'm just kidding of course, but seriously, nice.

People think about regret. Maybe it's only a small second-guessing of our choices, but that's close to the same thing. You can get lost in the past, wondering if you should have made different decisions. Perhaps my life would be better if…? Before you lose any more sleep over a botched chance to improve your existence, check out my definitive list of regret.

Worth Regretting (aka′ – never live it down list)
- Sleeping with you husband's brother
- Never expressing your dying love to that special person
- Telling your parents you hate them while running away
- Not taking a job you might love
- Not ending a bad relationship
- Beating a child
- Slapping your spouse
- Not burying the hatchet after a falling out with a friend
- Thinking she wouldn't have VD
- Hitting "reply all" on a private office rant
- That private video that got posted online
- Pirating Nickelback music
- Being a Mets fan (publicly)
- Being a fan of the Kardashians

Not too big a deal (Regret-me-nots)
- Sleeping with your wife's sister (oh wait, that's bad, isn't it?)
- Clogging the McDonald's toilet and not fessing up
- Pirating a new song release
- Sneaking into a 2nd movie
- Epic fail with a new hair style
- Beating a mime
- Slapping your spouse's ass (you thought they might like it)
- Forgetting to feed your goldfish as an 8-year-old
- Buying stock in LaserDisc
- Ranting anonymously online
- Admitting you like Coldplay
- Thinking Darius Rucker's real name was Hootie
- Holding out hope that Nick Cage would make a good film
- Thinking Tracy Chapman was a dude

I'm sure there could be more, but you likely understand my point. Having regrets is different from acknowledging poor choices. The moment you begin to regret your choices, you begin to question your future choices and before you know it, you've listened to Nickelback music again. Dammit! I though you knew better by now. You have no one to blame but yourself.

Technically speaking, I'm probably veering off towards remorse more than regret in much of this discussion, but many use these words interchangeably, even if wrong in doing so. What causes our negative feelings towards the choices we make? Is it a question solely of outcome? If that were the case, perhaps we'd like the opportunity to make every choice as perfect as can be. I think it would be hard to draw the line at one or two decisions. Sure, that trip to Vegas could have ended differently, but they can laser bad tattoos and you've still got the story – or at least what you can remember of it. Selfishly, I'll bet that most of the regrets that people would share revolve around choices that could have made their own lives better. What about the decisions that impacted others more than yourself? Perhaps those decisions, words said, or sentiments not shared are the ones that hold a greater sense of remorse. Looking out for yourself first is natural. I'm not even saying it's bad or wrong. I'm saying that we all do it, by and large. Those that do not are special, and are far better than I am.

My wife and I don't have kids, yet. Perhaps we will, but as the years pass by, it seems less likely. I don't have any regrets or feel any remorse for potentially not having children.

Author's Note: I took my sweet ass time writing this book over a decade, and the opportunity for kids long since passed us by. I got snipped a while back and I think it's funnier that I still left the first part of this paragraph in the book.

Am I second guessing it? Hell yes. Every, single, damn day.

Author's Note: Nope. That thought process has changed as well. I don't second guess it. In fact, I feel better about the decision each day. Every, single, damn day.

Our closest friends all have children. Children everywhere. They're spitting out kids like you've gotten them wet and then fed them after midnight (That's a movie reference. I'm not helping you if you don't know). I have no offspring to carry down my family name generations, but I really don't care. Williams is a common name anyway and my wife didn't even change her name. Funny side note on the last name - I was an ass the first time we crossed that bridge, somehow thinking it was necessary for her to give up her name for mine. I have no idea why it bothered me. I got over it pretty quick, but not before I'd made a fool of myself over the topic. Still not something I regret, but not something I'm all that proud of. Back to the children topic – it's a big example of life decisions where the consequences seem large in the scope of one's life, but small when examined in a larger scale. There is a large part of me that would've liked to have children to raise, teach, love and see grow into fine people of the next generation. I know that being Godparents (we have lots o' Godchildren) isn't nearly the same as having munchkins of our own. But, it doesn't mean that I cannot lead a full life without having children. My wife and I continue to move forward without the worries of "what if," not on only on the topic of procreation, but with our lives in general. Ask yourself, can you say the same? Are you confident, by and large, with your daily decisions?

If not, it's time for the tiniest fraction of introspection. You cannot live your life wallowing in regret. You cannot live wondering what might have been. If you've digested some of what is in the book, the common thread is that we're all a little messed up. Even the best of us has the worst of days. If you've screwed up in the past, of course you are living with the results. But is does not preclude you from trying to move forward positively. You may not have the ability to pull it off, but you have the right to try. I believe that we tend to look at regret in absolute terms. Here's an anecdotal - For Example: I went to high school with a couple guys who decided to make some counterfeit $20 bills. They spent that money at the cafeteria, and subsequently got caught doing so after a bit.

One of them lost college scholarship offers as a result. For a kid in their teens, that's a steep price to pay. Because of the consequences, his life track was significantly altered. I think it's safe to say that if you had asked him in the first few years that followed, "Do you regret trying to spend counterfeit money on cheese fries and pizza at the risk of losing a scholarship to an elite Division 1 school," the answer would have been a sobering "Yes, of course."

And in a world of "what if," that very well may be his answer today. But then again, maybe not. We've both been removed from high school over well over 20 years. This gentleman was a bright, intelligent young man. There's no reason to think that he didn't still get a good college education, a great job, and do fine in life. He simply may have started at community college instead of running track as a student athlete for Duke. Maybe he stayed closer to home and met the love of his life because of it. And maybe that poor decision as a teenager became such a powerful learning moment that he was better for it. At 18, his world was turned upside down. At 45, he's just another asshole trying to pay for his kid's college education wondering what the hell Snapchat is. He may still regret his actions, but likely much the way we regret not buying Bitcoin when that one crazy friend was talking it up years ago. "Look Andy – I have no idea what cryptocurrency is, and I'm not investing in virtual money, thank you very much."

Or maybe he never got over it. Maybe he leads a horrible life, got hooked on drugs and spends his days yelling at mailboxes for looking at him suspiciously. That's the problem with regret. If we live in the past, live in the "what if," then we cannot move forward. And you end up homeless, talking to squirrels about why clouds are following you. Too true.

• 36 •

Bubble wrap this fragile lesson

This book originally started as a way for me to vent without it being a journal. I like to tell stories. I'm generally considered a nice guy who keeps a level perspective on life. I live a normal life and am blessed with good health and good friends, great family and the best wife around (Of course I'm putting that part in. She'll be reading this stupid book too). I'm not a recovering alcoholic or drug addict with a great story of redemption. I can't tell you how to cope with addiction or help you find salvation. What I can tell you this book comes from the heart.

I hate self-help books. Not really, but kinda. I think the biggest problem I have with self-help gurus is an arrogance that comes along with thinking they know all the answers. It doesn't matter what stance they take. It's definitive, ego-driven, and generally full of crap. The advice is all encompassing, regardless of the variables that exist and the guidance is uniform despite the intricacies that separate your life from the next. My goal was to write against that frame of thought. If you're a grammar freak (and I may have mentioned that I was an English major in college), you'll hate this book. It's written with a complete lack of form and obedience to basic grammar. I wouldn't even categorize it as prose. In fact, here's a few, extra, commas, to, prove, a, point (It sort of looks that Shatner wrote that last sentence). I use fragments, words like "like" and edit my profanity only partially and most assuredly in an inconsistent manner. I want you to read this as if we are having a conversation and you aren't reading a medical journal or having my thoughts simply thrown at you.

My goal was to have some fun putting together the anti-self-help guide to living, thing. I understood the hypocritical beauty in offering advice in a book that mocks advice books. In the time that it has taken me to put this hot mess of words together, that irony has never been funnier than now as I try to find a way to wrap it all up poetically. It has done nothing but fuel my need to finish the book even though I went for months (or longer) on end without writing a single word. I purposely left out most of the elements that might leave a time stamp on the book. I didn't really want it to appear dated for fear it might lose its appeal. But after re-reading the book several times, it's clear that most of my references will be dated in some way. Oh well – makes for some extra Googling on your part. You want to know exactly how long it actually took me to write this? The answer is simply too many years. For this dribble? Are you kidding? I have several little books going, but like many people, I just dabble. It's tough to find the time to sit down and write, edit, publish, etc. I sure somebody could've knocked this out in a long weekend if they tried. I didn't know what I was doing, but if you're reading this now, apparently, I've figured it out. Kinda.

So, stay with me through these final paragraphs.

Life is busy and complicated. We have responsibilities, work, families that need our attention. We have our own drama, our own struggles, and our own problems. We have our insecurities, our baggage, and sometimes other people's baggage. From natural disasters to the one's we create for ourselves, life presents daily challenges. Take the moments available to live a full life, a fulfilling life. But he's the catch. I'm NOT saying carpe diem, in a way that has you chucking responsibility out the window. Nor am I saying that you should squeeze every second of every minute to up your productivity. I'm saying quite the opposite. If you want to watch Netflix and sit around playing on your phone, go for it. Yes, I know you should probably get at least one load of laundry going, but eventually you'll do it. It doesn't hurt to be a responsible adult, but you also need to recharge the batteries from time to time. You can binge watch Game of Thrones for the 5th time or you can be an over-achiever and try and teach yourself French. That's sorta gay, but go ahead.

Author's Note: *To all my gay friends – before you get all bent out of shape about that last remark, remember, I know some of "you" people.*

Author's Follow up: Okay – to all that were offended by the "you" people remark, let me remind you that I said it was "sorta gay," not like totally gay.

Author's Clarification: It has been brought to my attention – I was very much wrong in my initial labeling of learning French. It is not "sorta gay" as I'd previously and insensitively stated. It is not gay if it's some chick learning it.

Author's Explanation: I apologize to any women offended by the "chick" comment. I was wrong for even writing that. To play the different sexes card shows ignorance on my part. You are correct. It's pretty gay regardless of gender.

Author's Epiphany: Using homophobic language/slurs in any capacity is offensive and unacceptable in today's culture. I am wrong for having used it, even in a sarcastic comedic attempt. It was a faux pas on my part. See, that's French.

I had a whole section that was deleted on mass shootings. I scrapped it because in America, we've gone beyond Columbine. We've gone beyond Sandy Hook, beyond Virginia Tech, Orlando, Vegas, Stoneman Douglas. Sadly, the list goes on and on. I was trying to make a point that in the wake of tragedy, people jump to the cliche of saying "Make each day count as if it's your last," or "Live life to the fullest." That's horseshit advice. If you really knew it was your last day, you'd go absolutely nuts with reckless abandon. You cannot live that way. The overwhelming probability is that there most certainly is a tomorrow. And now you must face the consequences for crapping on your boss's desk because you "were living each day to the fullest." We live in a messed-up world where horrible things happen to good people. It would be fantastic if this weren't the case, but it is. It just clearly is. But that doesn't mean we don't carry on.

I'm all for living a fruitful life. I think it's generally good for people to venture out and try new things. You should make the most out of your short time here, or at least, make as much as you want to make of it. For the last time, you got that? Everyone must find their own path in life. We cannot live behind cliché. We cannot live in fear of losing people to tragedy. We cannot bubble wrap each other or save everyone from a terrible existence. Shit happens in war torn countries and third world cesspools. It happens in nice backyards and even in our brains. What you can do is listen for the chance to capture moments along this amazing journey from time to time. We can accept who we are. We can accept our faults. We can work to strengthen relationships, or part from unhealthy ones. We can grow and learn and love.

I wish the best to everyone that has read this book. Thanks for sticking with me. Please feel free to pass my thoughts along to anyone that needs some direction in this world. I hope when life gets tough and you need a reality check, you can turn to this book for a bit of levity have a little laugh. After all, this is a self-help book and all of life's answers are contained within these pages. That's a fact. I promise.